GREEK MYTHS

RETOLD BY ANN TURNBULL

ILLUSTRATED BY SARAH YOUNG

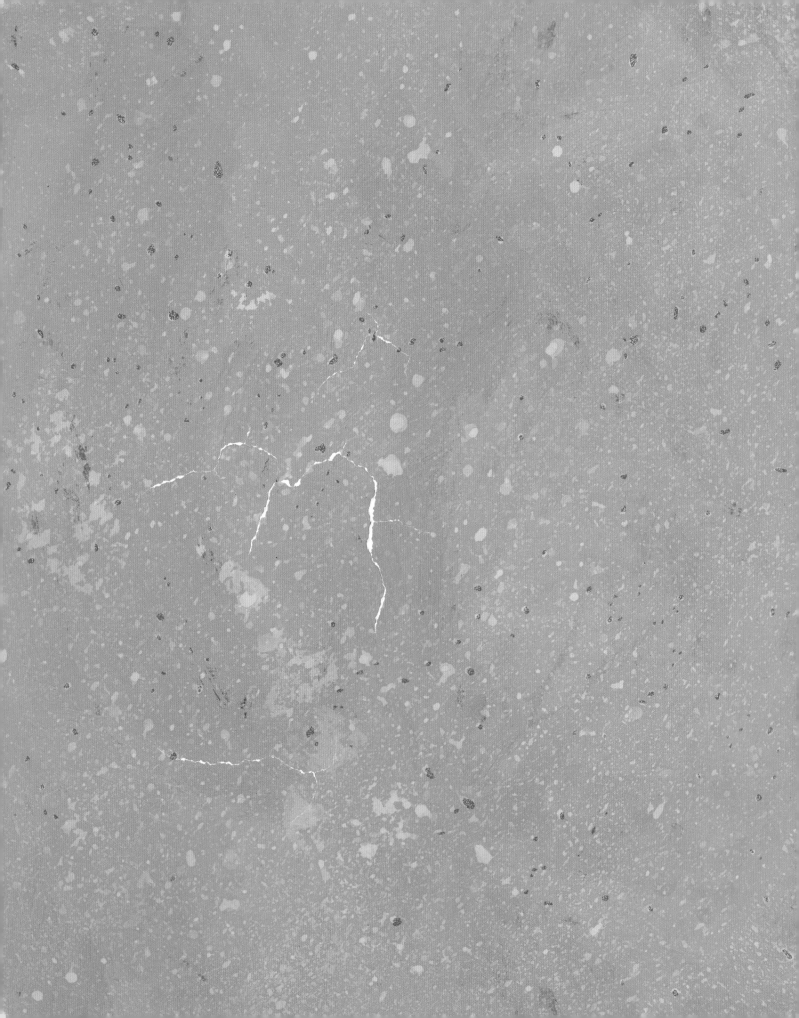

GREEK MYTHS

RETOLD BY ANN TURNBULL

ILLUSTRATED BY SARAH YOUNG

WALKER BOOKS
AND SUBSIDIARIES
LONDON · BOSTON · SYDNEY · AUCKLAND

I N T R O D

 My father introduced me to the Greek myths when I was a child. His favourites were Homer's epics. He loved them for their humour and their evocation of a bright, golden world. I was captivated by Pan and by the mysterious nymphs, fauns and satyrs, the spirits of woods and streams. I liked the way they could change shape, go from woman to tree, god to river, so that life and nature became one.

To the earliest people, the whole land – rocks, trees, rivers, caves, springs – was alive and inhabited by nature spirits. Tmolus was a god but also a mountain. Arethusa, a nymph with human form, could turn into a stream and emerge as a new spring. Pegasus, the winged horse, created springs with a stamp of his hoof. Hades lived in the Underworld and burst forth from fiery fissures in the earth.

U C T I O N

The gods of ancient Greece were immortal. The first gods were the Titans, who gave birth to the twelve Olympians – the gods who feature in these stories. Mount Olympus was believed to be their home. They are the gods who can be seen on the Parthenon frieze, and their names are Aphrodite, Apollo, Ares, Artemis, Athena, Demeter, Dionysus, Hephaestus, Hera, Hermes, Poseidon and Zeus.

The Muses were the daughters of Zeus and Mnemosyne (Memory). They were the goddesses who inspired poets, musicians and philosophers, and Homer calls on the Muse to speak through him when he begins his story of Odysseus. There were nine Muses: Kalliope (epic poetry), Klio (history), Euterpe (music), Terpsichore (dancing), Erato (lyric poetry), Melpomene (tragedy), Thalia (comedy), Polyhymnia (sacred song) and Urania (astronomy). Our word "museum" comes from the Muses.

Unlike humans, with their short, fragile lives, nymphs and other nature spirits were long-lived, though not immortal. Nymphs were the spirits of springs, trees, caves and the sea. Dryads and Oreiades were tree nymphs; they lived in the mountains, where most of the forests grew. Often a tree nymph would be born with her tree and die when the tree died. Naiads were water nymphs and Nereids were sea nymphs. Satyrs and silens were wild men of the woods, part human, part animal. They were often followers of Dionysus, the god of wine, and were clever and mischievous.

In this collection you will find a mixture of nature myths, hero tales and stories of struggle between gods and mortals. I have left out Odysseus and the Trojan War epics because these are separate story-cycles that deserve a book of their own. The more myths I read, the more I realized

how many of them link together. Some stories, like Arachne, stand alone, but many others lead on one to another. In particular, the story of the Minotaur leads directly to Ariadne on Naxos.

I have tried to go back to early versions of the myths, those collected and rewritten by the ancient Greek poets and historians, so you will find that King Midas does not have a daughter and that Pandora opens a jar, not a box. The Romans gave the Greek gods different names (for example, Aphrodite became Venus), but in these stories the Greek names are always used. The spellings are mostly the more familiar ones, except that I have used "K" instead of "C" in names like Kalydon. Greek names are easy to pronounce if you remember that a final "e" (as in Aphrodite) is always sounded (Afroditey).

Ann Turnbull

C · O · N · T

11 **EARTH, THE HEAVENS AND THE UNDERWORLD**

13 ARETHUSA

19 PERSEPHONE

29 ORPHEUS AND EURYDICE

37 PHAETHON AND THE CHARIOT OF THE SUN

47 **MONSTERS AND HEROES**

49 THE MINOTAUR

63 ARIADNE ON NAXOS

71 THE KALYDONIAN BOAR HUNT

E · N · T · S

ATALANTA'S RACE   82

PERSEUS AND THE GORGON'S HEAD   91

BELLEROPHON AND THE WINGED HORSE   108

GODS AND MORTALS   119

PAN AND SYRINX   121

KING MIDAS AND THE GOLDEN TOUCH   127

KING MIDAS AND THE MUSIC CONTEST   137

ARACHNE   145

ECHO AND NARCISSUS   153

PANDORA   161

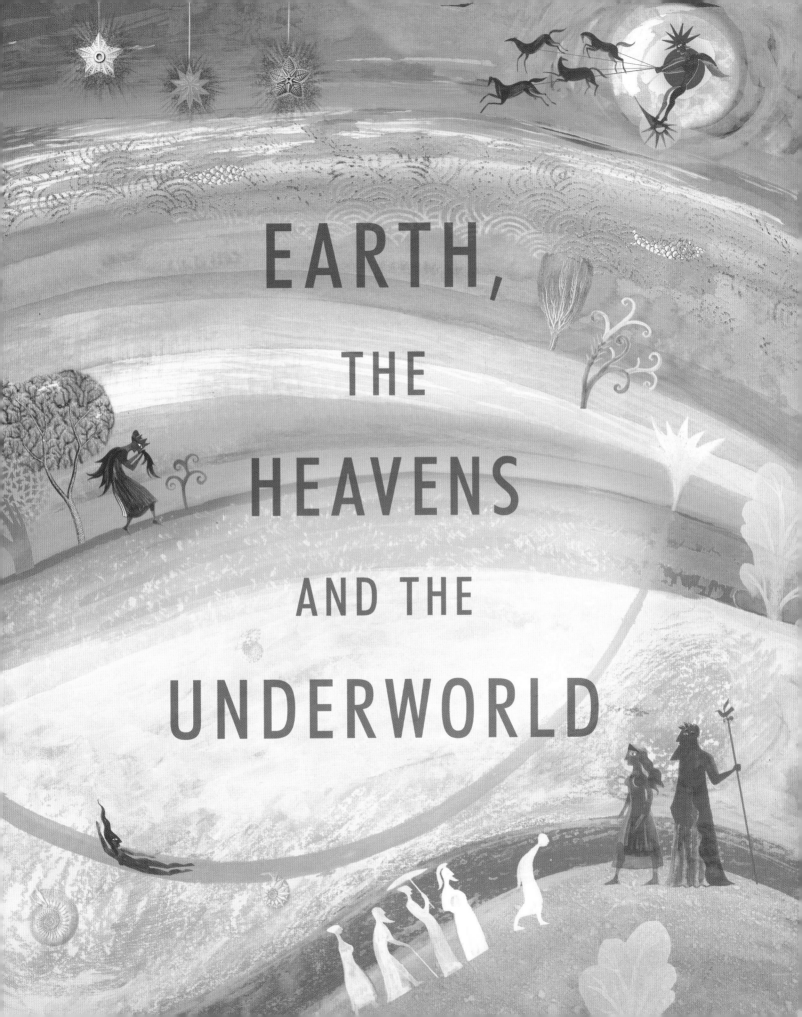

EARTH, THE HEAVENS AND THE UNDERWORLD

ARETHUSA

Arethusa was one of the nymphs who served Artemis, the virgin goddess of the hunt. She was beautiful, but cared nothing for her beauty; all her joy was in hunting with bow and arrow and roaming the woods and hills and rocky crags of Elis and Arcadia.

One burning day Arethusa, hot from the hunt, found herself alone on a bank beside the River Alpheus, where willow trees overhung the water. The cool water, dark with shade, seemed to invite her. She took off her clothes, plunged in, swam, twisted, splashed and dived and rose up with dripping hair.

As she dived a second time she heard a rumbling sound and felt a force in the water moving towards her. Alarmed, she swam for the bank and

climbed out – and turned to see the river god Alpheus emerge, streaming water, in human form.

Arethusa ran. But the god, struck by her beauty, had fallen in love. He pursued her. The nymph was fleet and strong, and she ran like a hunted animal. She dodged, hid, only to break from cover and run again. Still Alpheus gained on her. At last her strength gave out, and she cried aloud to Artemis, "Save me, great goddess!"

The goddess heard her. She hid Arethusa in a cloud of mist. Inside it, the nymph stood trembling while Alpheus prowled outside, around and around, balked and puzzled. He knew Arethusa was near, because her footprints stopped and did not come out on the other side; and so he waited, while the nymph shook with fear.

Now Artemis saw that her nymph could not escape, so she caused her to dissolve into drops of water. Water streamed from Arethusa's hair and down her body, and out from under her feet; and in a moment she had become a stream, trickling out from the cloud of mist and down the hillside, away from Alpheus.

But the god knew that stream; he recognized Arethusa; and he changed back into his own river form and was about to engulf her when Artemis cleft the earth and opened up a chasm – and Arethusa plunged into it and flowed deep down under the earth.

Through caves and twisting passages Arethusa travelled in darkness, under earth and sea. And as she fled she glimpsed, in the shadows, the

cold king of the Underworld, Hades, and beside him a young girl, his bride, crowned with a diadem. The girl was pale, and Arethusa saw in her eyes a fear like her own.

Driven by that fear, she flowed on through caverns beneath the sea until she came to the coast of Sicily; and there, on the island of Ortygia, she burst forth as a fountain of fresh water, forming a new spring.

There she stayed, as Naiad of that spring. The people of Sicily brought offerings to her; and some say that in time Alpheus, his love unquenched, found his way at last across the sea and mingled his waters with hers.

PERSEPHONE

Persephone was the daughter of Demeter, the corn goddess. Demeter caused the crops to grow and the harvest to ripen, and taught men how to plough and tend the earth. She was one of the Olympians, the sister of Zeus, and she had a shrine at Enna in the centre of Sicily.

Long ago, when Zeus had defeated the monster Typhon, he had bound and buried him under Mount Etna in Sicily. There the giant writhed and struggled to escape, and sometimes he burst open the earth's crust, sending hot ash and streams of molten lava flowing across the land. Hades, the god of the Underworld, felt these disturbances and feared lest the earth should crack and daylight seep into his dark realm to terrify the spirits of the dead. He rode out in his golden chariot drawn by four black horses to inspect the foundations of his kingdom.

There, in the upper world of light and growth, he came upon Persephone among a company of nymphs, gathering flowers in a meadow. The air was sweet with the scent of lilies, of violets, crocus and irises, and the girls laughed and chattered as they ran about with armfuls of blossoms and piled them into baskets.

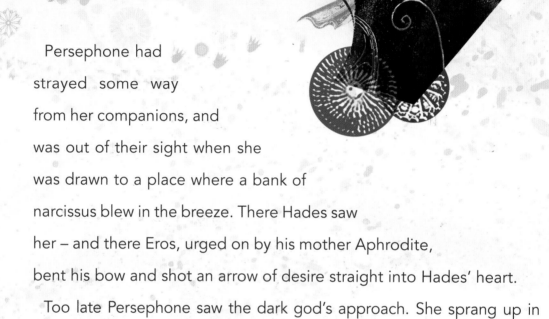

Persephone had strayed some way from her companions, and was out of their sight when she was drawn to a place where a bank of narcissus blew in the breeze. There Hades saw her – and there Eros, urged on by his mother Aphrodite, bent his bow and shot an arrow of desire straight into Hades' heart.

Too late Persephone saw the dark god's approach. She sprang up in terror – tried to run – struggled as he seized her, dragged her into his chariot, and whipped up the horses. Persephone screamed. The nymphs heard her, and from far off her mother, the goddess, heard her too, but no one saw what had happened. Hades drove his chariot across the fields of Enna, crushing flowers, scattering flocks of frightened goats. Persephone clung on and cried for help; but Hades gathered speed. Across Sicily he drove, over mountains and lakes and plains, through

sulphurous Palica, past Syracuse – until he was forced to stop at the River Kyane, where the Naiad of that place caused her waters to rise up in protest. But the Naiad was no match for a god. Hades struck the water with his sceptre and at once the river bed split and opened up a chasm that led straight to the Underworld. Now Persephone saw what was to be her fate. As the chariot plunged down, the desperate girl pulled off her golden sash and threw it into the river; then the earth closed over her.

In the world above, Demeter searched everywhere for her daughter. She lit pine torches in the fires of Mount Etna, and for nine days and nights she did not rest, nor wash; she did not taste ambrosia nor drink nectar; she roamed the world crying out her daughter's name, asking everyone she met for news of Persephone. But there was none. Demeter neglected the crops. Corn withered in the fields; cattle died, and the people went hungry. The goddess cared for nothing but her daughter; in her grief and fear for her child she was inconsolable.

At last, having searched the world for Persephone, she returned to Sicily – and there, cast up on the bank of the River Kyane, she found her daughter's golden sash.

As she held it, muddy and stained from the water, Demeter knew for certain that Persephone had been taken by force. She howled and tore her hair and cursed the land as ungrateful and undeserving of the gift of grain. She broke the ploughs, caused hot sun to scorch the seeds, violent rain and wind to scatter them, flocks of hungry birds to devour any that were left. She wandered, ragged and grieving, across Sicily, and sat down at last by the fountain of Arethusa at Ortygia and wept.

Arethusa, the Naiad of that spring, rose waist-high from the water and tossed back her dripping hair.

"Immortal goddess," she said, "do not blame the earth for your daughter's loss. It opened against its will to take her into the Underworld. But she is not dead."

And she told Demeter how, as she fled the amorous river god Alpheus in caverns deep below the earth, she had seen Persephone, the bride of Hades: "sorrowing still, and full of fear; and yet a queen, ruler of that dark land, and worthy consort of a great god."

"Persephone? My daughter? Queen of the Underworld?"

Now Demeter was filled with anger against the gods. She rose to Olympus to protest – for Hades was her brother: when the realms were divided up, Zeus was given sovereignty over heaven and earth, Poseidon became ruler of the seas and oceans, and Hades became Lord of the Underworld, the kingdom of the dead.

Demeter burst in upon the gods, and her fury was terrifying.

"Hades has stolen my daughter! He has taken her against her will! I demand justice from the gods!"

Zeus tried to calm her. "Sister," he said, "Hades is an immortal, a deathless god. He has made your daughter a queen. You should rejoice."

But Demeter did not rejoice. She insisted on Persephone's return. Until then, she said, she would mourn and the land would be untended and the people would starve.

When the gods saw that Demeter would not be reconciled to the loss of her daughter, they sent Hermes to bring Persephone home.

"On one condition," said Zeus. "That while she has been in the Underworld she has taken no food or drink. This is the rule the Fates decreed long ago and I cannot change it."

And so Hermes hurried on swift feet to Hades' kingdom, while Demeter waited in her temple at Enna, full of hope and fear.

She was right to be afraid. Hades, anxious not to lose his beautiful bride, had cut in half a red-fleshed pomegranate and offered it to the girl. Persephone knew she should not eat or drink, but she was thirsty, and the fruit tempted her. She took three seeds and ate them.

Then Hades knew Persephone was bound to him for ever; so when Hermes came to claim her, he let her go, knowing she must return.

Demeter, waiting in her temple, saw Hermes and Persephone coming from far off. She cried out, "Persephone! My daughter!" – and ran like a maenad down the mountainside and clasped Persephone in her arms and kissed her.

"Tell me," she said, searching her daughter's face, "tell me you have neither eaten nor drunk in Hades' realm?"

Persephone could not look her mother in the eye. "I did not mean to," she said, "but I was thirsty, and it was so little – only three pomegranate seeds."

"Then you are lost!" cried Demeter. With foreboding in her heart she accompanied Hermes and Persephone to Olympus, and found Hades already there.

"Persephone is mine," said Hades. "The Fates decree it."

"I cannot deny your right," agreed Zeus, "but her mother grieves and mankind suffers."

He ruled that Persephone should live in the world above for two-thirds of every year, but that for the third part she must return to the Underworld as Hades' queen.

And so it came to be. When her daughter was in the Underworld, Demeter mourned. The earth grew cold and barren and the grain lay dormant. But when Persephone returned, the days began to lengthen; flowers bloomed and the trees put out new leaves, and people knew that spring had come again.

ORPHEUS

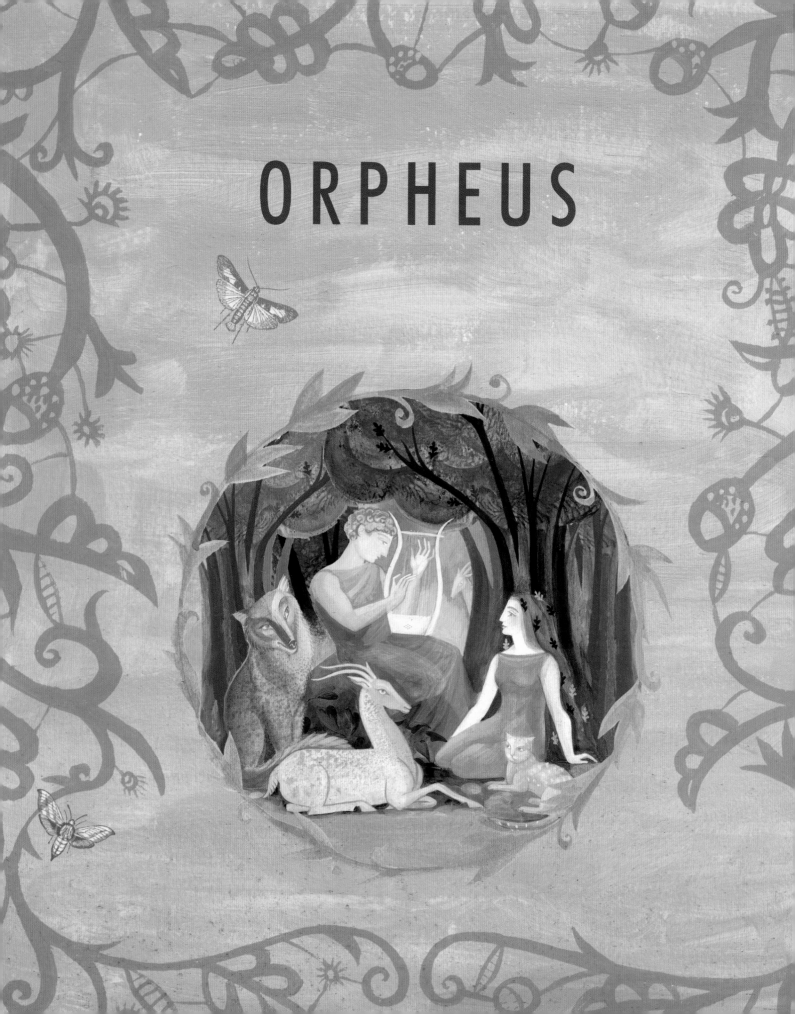

AND EURYDICE

Orpheus was the son of a king and the muse Kalliope. The god Apollo gave him a lyre and the Muses taught him to play and sing. His voice was so sweet that he could enchant the birds and beasts, and all nature delighted in his music. Wild cats and wolves came out of their lairs to hear him; mountain goats sprang down from the heights; trees bowed their heads as he passed, and even rocks moved from their places.

Orpheus lived in Thrace, a land of high, snow-topped mountains, forests and waterfalls. Every river, every stream, every tree and cave had its nymph – the spirit and guardian of the place. One day, as Orpheus sat playing his lyre beneath an oak tree, he looked up into the leaves and saw a nymph sitting on a branch high above him in the dappled shade. Her feet were bare and her long hair was braided with oak leaves, and she smiled as she watched and listened to him. When he called to her, she came down. She told him her name was Eurydice. Orpheus fell in love with her, and after that first meeting he came every day to her tree to sing and win her love.

When Orpheus and Eurydice were married, the nymphs of river and forest danced at their wedding and all nature rejoiced in their happiness.

But Eurydice was so beautiful that other men desired her. One day she was walking by a riverside when she was waylaid by the god Aristaeus. Aristaeus tried to seize Eurydice, but she escaped him and fled through the meadows. It was summertime and the grass was long, and as she ran Eurydice stepped on a snake which reared up and bit her. At once she collapsed. She felt the deadly venom flowing through her veins and cried out, and the nymphs of the forest heard her and called her name. Their cries passed from one to another: "Eurydice is dying! Dying!" and all the hills echoed with their wails. Orpheus heard them and raced

to the meadow, but by the time he reached her, Eurydice was dead.

Orpheus was inconsolable. He vowed he could not live without Eurydice and would go to the Underworld to fetch her back.

But to reach the Underworld he must first cross four great rivers. The last of these was the Styx, which was guarded by Charon, the ferryman. Only the dead could cross the Styx, but Orpheus sang and played, and his music charmed the ferryman and melted his heart; he rowed Orpheus across the river to the gates of the Underworld. Here Orpheus came upon the three-headed dog, Cerberus, who growled

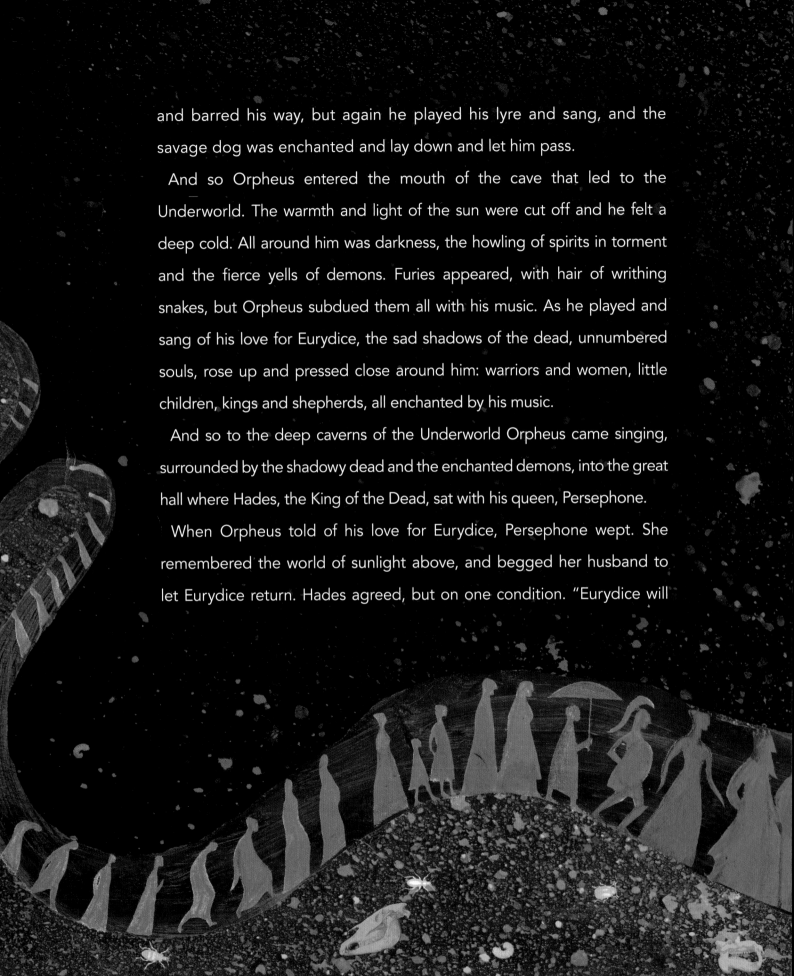

and barred his way, but again he played his lyre and sang, and the savage dog was enchanted and lay down and let him pass.

And so Orpheus entered the mouth of the cave that led to the Underworld. The warmth and light of the sun were cut off and he felt a deep cold. All around him was darkness, the howling of spirits in torment and the fierce yells of demons. Furies appeared, with hair of writhing snakes, but Orpheus subdued them all with his music. As he played and sang of his love for Eurydice, the sad shadows of the dead, unnumbered souls, rose up and pressed close around him: warriors and women, little children, kings and shepherds, all enchanted by his music.

And so to the deep caverns of the Underworld Orpheus came singing, surrounded by the shadowy dead and the enchanted demons, into the great hall where Hades, the King of the Dead, sat with his queen, Persephone.

When Orpheus told of his love for Eurydice, Persephone wept. She remembered the world of sunlight above, and begged her husband to let Eurydice return. Hades agreed, but on one condition. "Eurydice will follow you out of the Underworld," he said, "but you must not look back, or speak to her, until you are both once more in the world of men."

Orpheus was overjoyed. He looked about him, hoping to see Eurydice among the shades who thronged the hall, but Persephone said, "She will follow. You will not see Eurydice until you return to the sunlight."

So Orpheus began the journey back to the light. The way was long and lonely. Hades had promised him that Eurydice would follow, but he heard no sound of anyone behind him. Sometimes as he climbed on and upwards he stopped and listened for her. Perhaps, he thought, he would hear the rustle of her robe, or her soft breath, or the light tread of her feet. But all he heard was his own breathing and, when he moved again, his own footsteps. A whisper of doubt entered his mind. Had the gods deceived him? But perhaps she is too far behind for me to hear her, he thought, and he moved on, trying to believe that his beloved wife was with him in the shadows, stepping in his footsteps.

At last light began to penetrate: a greyish light that showed Orpheus the

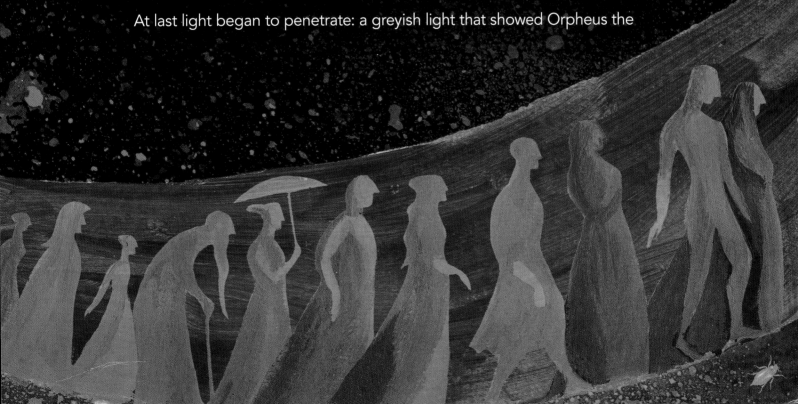

clustering shades of the dead, the stones under his feet, the rugged walls on either side. A faint sweet air came from far ahead: the breath of summer. Soon he would enter the world of the living, but was Eurydice behind him? He could not bear to return alone. He listened again: nothing.

Oh, speak to me, Eurydice, he thought. Make some sound so that I know you are there!

He began to fear that Hades had deceived him, that he was the victim of a cruel trick. The urge to turn round and look was almost overwhelming, but he went on, up into the air that smelt of thyme and pine resin, where the shades of the dead faded away and he saw ahead of him, framed in the cave entrance, the bright world of men.

As he reached that divide, and the warmth of the sun received him, he could bear it no longer. He was overcome with fear that she was not there, that the invisible barrier between the two worlds would separate them.

He glanced over his shoulder.

And Eurydice was there! He saw her, fair and full of life: her sweet face, smiling lips, flowing hair, the joy on her face as she approached the light – and then, in the next instant, all colour vanished; her skin turned ashen, and it seemed that some great force was pulling her back, away from him.

He cried out in terror, "Eurydice!"

And the nymph wailed, "Oh, Orpheus, what have you done? You have lost me! The Fates call me back — "

"Take my hand, Eurydice!"

"I cannot see! All is dark, dark..."

She stretched out her hands, and he almost reached them, almost touched her, before the dark power triumphed. He saw her eyes close, her arms fall limp, her body fade to a shadow and disappear like smoke.

"Eurydice!" he cried again; and in the caverns of the Underworld the echo of her name mocked him as it died away.

Now Orpheus knew the full force of his folly and his lack of faith. He rushed forward, and would have followed Eurydice straight back to the Underworld, but Charon came and stood across the way; and this time no pleading, no music that Orpheus could make would soften the guardian's heart.

Then Orpheus knew that he had lost Eurydice for ever.

He left the forest where he had lived with her and went north to the cold mountains. For years he played his lyre and sang in the icy caverns and wept for his lost wife. Many nymphs offered him their love, but he would have no other. He never again looked at another woman, and because of this the wild women of Thrace were insulted and angry, for they thought his grief had gone on too long. His end came one night when they pursued and killed him, and tore him in pieces and scattered his body across the land. But the Muses mourned him. They gathered his remains and buried them below Mount Olympus, in a place where nightingales sang over his grave.

PHAETHON AND THE CHARIOT OF THE SUN

Phaethon's story begins in Ethiopia, where he lived with his sisters, his mother Klymene and his step-father Merops. When Phaethon became a youth, his mother told him that his true father was Helios, the sun god. Phaethon was filled with awe and pride at this news. He boasted to his friends of his immortal lineage, but they mocked him, calling his mother a liar and him a fool for believing her.

Phaethon, hurt and angry, went to his mother and told her how he had stood silent, stung by the taunts, but unable to refute them.

"Give me some proof," he begged, "some token that I can show!"

Klymene was moved by his request and angry at the insult to herself. She flung out her arms and held them up to heaven. "Look up," she cried, "at the great shining glory in the sky! I swear to you that he who shines down on you now is your father. If I lie, may I never see his light again!"

Phaethon threw his arms around her and said, "I never doubted you, Mother! But give me proof!"

"For that," said Klymene, "you must travel east, to the place where the sun rises, and ask your father to acknowledge you as his son. Go – for I see your heart is set on it."

Phaethon wasted no time. He set off at once, through Ethiopia and across India, to the home of Helios, his father, and stood, at last, awe-struck before the palace of the sun god.

This palace was a wonder. Its soaring columns gleamed with gold, reflecting back the sun's fire; the doors were silver, the pediments inset with ivory. All around its walls were carved gods and nymphs: the sea gods, the gods of sky and earth, satyrs and centaurs, nymphs of woods and rivers. And on the silver doors, six on each, were engraved the twelve signs of the Zodiac.

These doors opened, and Phaethon, trembling now, passed through into the presence of the god.

He stood blinking, dazzled by the light, and shielded his eyes with one hand. From between his fingers he glimpsed Helios, draped in purple, seated on a golden throne and with a radiant crown upon his head. All around him, each in her place, stood the Days, the Months, the Years, and the Hours. The Seasons were there: Spring, crowned with flowers; brown Summer garlanded with grain; rich Autumn; and icy Winter.

Helios knew Phaethon at once. He turned his shining countenance towards the youth and asked, "What is it that brings my son here?"

Phaethon, overjoyed to be called "son", exclaimed, "Father! Great Helios! My mother spoke truth! Give me proof, I beg you, that I am indeed your son – some sign that everyone will know."

Helios held out his arms and embraced the youth before the assembled company.

"Your mother did speak truth, and you deserve to be called my son," he said. "Ask what you will. I will give whatever you desire."

No sooner had he spoken than Phaethon replied, "Let me drive the chariot of the sun for one day through the heavens! Let me control its fiery horses, and let all men see me and know that I am the son of Helios!"

Then the god regretted his rash promise. Grief and fear overwhelmed him – but he had given his word. Yet still he sought to discourage the eager boy.

"Choose again!" he cautioned him. "This is the one thing I would deny you. You are too young, too slight – and a mere mortal. Even the great gods do not aspire to drive my chariot. Not one of them – not even Zeus himself – could manage my team of horses, nor hold my chariot on its true course. Choose again, my son, I beg you."

But Phaethon held fast to his desire. Nothing his father said could change it. And so, with sorrow in his heart, the sun god agreed. "Dawn approaches," he said. "We must make ready."

Phaethon looked out and saw the moon fading as the rosy light of dawn

grew in the east. The Hours went to yoke the horses. Helios placed his own golden helmet on Phaethon's head, and over it he set a crown of sunbeams that flashed in the morning light. He dressed the youth in the white kilt and golden robe of the sun god, and laced the purple boots upon his feet.

"Listen, my child," he said. "My horses are eager; they will race across the heavens. Do not use the whip, but rein them – rein them hard. Follow a course that curves between the Poles, neither too high nor too low. Let the morning star lead you, and you will not go astray."

He led Phaethon out to where the horses of the sun waited behind the gates of dawn; four fire-breathing horses, eager to be gone. Helios led him to them one by one and told him their names: Aethon, Eous, Pyrois and Phlegon – Blaze, Dawn, Fire and Flame. They neighed and tossed their manes, and their stamping hooves struck sparks from the floor.

"Choose again, my son," begged Helios. "There is still time."

But Phaethon, all alight with joy and gratitude, kissed his father, sprang into the chariot and seized the reins. The Hours flung wide the gates of dawn, and the horses leapt up into the sky.

They raced above the clouds, high, higher, into the heavens – and Phaethon knew at once that he could never control them. They felt his light weight, his uncertain hand. The chariot leapt and jolted; the horses, unchecked, left the sun's pathway. Phaethon was helpless with fear. He could neither rein in the horses nor find the true road. The chariot veered

to the North Pole – warming the icy Bear, who fled enraged across the skies – then swung south, running wild among the constellations.

Now Phaethon looked down from the height of heaven and saw below him – far, far below – the seas and continents spread out; and such dread gripped him that he could scarcely stand. He pulled on the reins; he tried to call to the horses, but in his panic he forgot their names. He wished with all his heart that he had heeded his father and had never chosen this course. But he could not turn back; and far ahead of him he

saw the west, the day's end, and knew he would never reach it.

New terrors rose before him. All across the dark sky he saw huge starry beasts that barred his way. The Scorpion's great claws curved towards him, its tail arching, poised to strike. In alarm he dropped the reins, and at once the horses swerved away across the sky, out of all control — first up to highest heaven, where they scorched the halls of the gods, then down to earth, so low that every mountain top burst into flame.

Phaethon saw green fields burn and turn to parched desert in an instant.

Deep cracks opened in the earth's crust, and Hades in his dark realm was roused to anger. Etna and Olympus burned. On every side the world was ablaze. Great cities were on fire, kingdoms and empires destroyed. Phaethon felt the chariot red-hot beneath his feet; he breathed in the fiery vapours. The earth's axis was jolted, the constellations flung from their places; Atlas, who supports the world on his shoulders, staggered under the sudden shift of weight.

Then seas and rivers began to disappear. The nymphs wailed in their dry springs. Small streams dried to cracked and dusty earth. Seas shrank; great sand banks appeared; seals and dolphins were stranded on the shores. From below the sea, Poseidon rose and roared in protest. Gaia, the earth goddess, her voice clogged with ash, called on Zeus: "Help us, great Zeus! Is the earth to die? Look at my burning mountains, the deserts where once men grew grain and olives, the dry springs and rivers where the nymphs mourn. Even the Poles are burning. Soon heaven itself will be destroyed."

Then Zeus rose to the height of heaven, to the place from which he cast his thunderbolts and lightning. He saw Phaethon, still clinging to the chariot as it careered above the earth. With a thunderbolt in his hand he took aim, threw, and struck. Phaethon was pitched in an instant out of the chariot and into death. The horses panicked, pulled against each other; the chariot broke apart, and burning wreckage flew across the sky.

And Phaethon, flames streaming from his hair, fell headlong, like a falling star, and plunged into the waters of the River Eridanos.

Then Helios, in grief, hid his bright face, and while he mourned the world was without sun. The only light came from the smouldering fires left by Phaethon's passing; and by this light Klymene and her daughters searched for the youth's body. They came at last to Italy and found that the nymphs of Eridanos had buried him beside the river and erected a stone in his memory:

"Here lies Phaethon, charioteer of the sun; who fell to earth, yet dared to reach for heaven."

Then Klymene clutched the stone and wept; and Phaethon's sisters wept for so long that at last they turned into weeping poplar trees.

But Zeus, in pity for Phaethon, whom he had been forced to destroy, raised the youth to the skies and fixed him as a constellation in heaven, where he is called the Charioteer.

MONSTERS
AND
HEROES

THE MINOTAUR

All around the Aegean Sea, people heard tales of the Minotaur – a man with the head and shoulders of a bull. Rumour told that the monster had been born to Pasiphae, the wife of King Minos of Crete, and that it lived in a maze of tunnels under the great palace of Knossos and fed on human flesh.

Minos, King of Crete, was master of the Aegean. He exacted tribute from all the surrounding city states, and the sight of his black-prowed ships sent terror into the hearts of the people.

The Athenians had especial cause to fear and hate him, for he demanded from them every year a tribute of seven youths and seven maidens. These young people, chosen by lot, were taken to Knossos and sent into the maze, one by one, to be devoured by the Minotaur.

For two years the Athenians sent this tribute, knowing that if they did not their city would be attacked and destroyed by the superior power of the

Cretans. They sent the victims in a ship with black sails to show their grief, and the parents and friends of those chosen wailed and tore their hair as the ship set sail. Their King, Aegeus, could do nothing to help them.

Then, in the third year, Aegeus' son, Theseus, came to Athens. He had grown up at Troezen with his mother, Aethra, daughter of the King of

Troezen, and now that he was come of age she had sent him to his father. Theseus had met with many dangers on his journey to Athens, and even when he reached his father's palace he was not safe, for Aegeus had married the sorceress Medea. Medea feared she would lose her power over Aegeus if Theseus was acknowledged as his son, so she tried to persuade

her husband to kill the young stranger, saying he was an impostor. But Aegeus recognized the sword that Theseus wore and knew this was truly his son. He welcomed him home and Medea was banished.

Soon after Aegeus was reunited with his son, the messenger came from Knossos, demanding seven youths and seven maidens. Once again, the citizens arranged for lots to be drawn. But Theseus said, "Father! Let only six youths be chosen by lot. I will be the seventh. And I promise you I will kill the Minotaur and bring the sons and daughters of Athens home, or die in the attempt."

Aegeus was horrified. He did not want his new-found son's name even to go into the lottery. But Theseus insisted.

"It is only right that I, the king's son, should go with our people," he said.

And so it was arranged. The lots were drawn, the youths and maidens chosen and sent with Theseus aboard a ship with black sails.

"If I return victorious," Theseus promised his father, "I will change the black sails for white, and you will see me coming across the sea, and rejoice."

When the ship from Athens arrived at Knossos, the fourteen youths and maidens were taken ashore and up to the great palace of Minos. There they were paraded before the king and his court. Because of his dress and manner, the Cretans knew that Theseus must be the Athenian king's son. The youth held his head high and gazed boldly at his captors. Beside Queen Pasiphae stood a girl – a princess – whose glance met his. The girl's eyes were dark and bright. Her brown hair was piled up and coiled at the back of her head and a single ringlet lay upon one bare shoulder. She wore a flounced dress edged with gold, and jewels flashed on her neck and arms.

There was no time for more than that brief glance before the prisoners were taken below and locked in a room to await their fate. Many of them were mere children and in great distress, crying for their mothers, but Theseus comforted them and told them he would offer to be first to go into the labyrinth.

"I have sworn to kill the Minotaur and bring you all safely home," he said.

They talked together of what they had heard about the labyrinth. King Minos had ordered his architect, Daedalus, to construct a maze so intricate, so full of twisting passages and dead ends, that no one who was sent in there would ever find his way out. Up and down those passages the Minotaur roamed at will. The victims would be shut in without light, food or water. They might evade the monster for

a while, perhaps hours, perhaps days, but in the end he would hunt them down and kill them.

And yet, thought Theseus, there must be a way to defeat the Minotaur.

He was pondering this when he heard low voices outside the room, and then the door was quietly unlocked and someone came in, veiled in a cloak.

Another prisoner, Theseus thought at first. But then the cloak was cast aside, and he saw the gleam of gold in the darkness and recognized the bright eyes of the princess he had seen in the hall above.

She singled out Theseus and drew him aside.

"I am Ariadne, daughter of Minos and sister to the Minotaur," she said. "I mean to help you escape." From under the cloak she brought a sword and a ball of thread and gave them to Theseus. "The Minotaur is strong but he is also heavy and slow. With this sword you can outwit and kill him. But when you enter the labyrinth be sure to unwind the thread behind you, otherwise you will never find your way out."

"Lady," said Theseus, "why do you do this?"

And yet he knew the reason, for he saw that Ariadne had fallen in love with him.

"I want you to live," said Ariadne. Her eyes shone. "Theseus, when you leave Knossos, take me with you! Take me to Athens as your bride!"

And Theseus agreed. Indeed, he could hardly refuse. And what a stroke that would be, he thought: to outwit Minos and steal his daughter into the bargain!

Ariadne left, and as dawn rose in the world above, the guards came to choose a prisoner to send into the labyrinth.

Theseus stood up.

"Let me be first," he said.

And so Theseus entered the labyrinth. As the door closed behind him he stood in such total darkness that it seemed to press upon his eyes. A smell of rotten flesh, of death and decay, came from the passage ahead of him; and from far off he heard bellowing, the voice of an enormous bull.

For a moment he was so afraid he could not move. But first, he knew, he must secure his escape. He took Ariadne's gift, the ball of thread, and tied the end to a nail on the great door behind him. Then he stepped into the darkness.

He began to feel his way forward, letting the twine pay out behind him. The smells were suffocating, the darkness threatening in its completeness. He could not advance with any speed. When he tried, he hit his hip and shoulder hard against rock and had to cast about, hands outstretched, to find which way the passage turned. He found it, moved steadily on for some way, then stepped on something soft, horrible, that had a bad smell. A corpse?

He edged past it, then came hard up against a wall. He felt all around. This time there was no turn, no break in the smooth rock face. It was a dead end. He retraced his steps.

The bellowing of the bull sounded closer now. He gripped the hilt of the sword. He would not allow himself to feel fear.

He moved on, in a direction that felt as if it was leading to the centre, where the bellowing came from. The thread dropped with a continuous faint rustle behind him as he turned first down one passage, then another. The darkness seemed to move back a little as his eyes grew accustomed to it, but still he could see nothing.

The ball of twine was growing smaller in his hand. What if it runs out, he thought? What if I am trapped here, at the centre of the maze?

The bellowing was loud. It reverberated among the passages, making it difficult for Theseus to judge its direction. But it was closer now, and with it came other sounds: snorts and snufflings, and eager grunts. The monster had sensed his presence.

Theseus rounded a twist in the walls and the stench of the beast came rushing towards him, and he knew it was there, hidden in the dark, at the end of the passage. He stood still. Could the Minotaur see? He was sure it had scented him. He heard it snuffling and questing; and then, with a great bellow, it was upon him.

He heard the rush of its weight and stepped aside deftly, letting it plunge on. But it had smelt him. It turned at once, came again; and he

knew its bull's head would be lowered, the horns curving towards his belly; he imagined how easily it could catch and toss and trample him. Beneath the bull's snorts he heard his own quick panting breath, and knew the Minotaur must hear it too.

If only he could see! As it charged he ducked – and felt the terrible strength of his opponent as a strong hand grasped him by the shoulder. He twisted away, ducked again, got behind the creature. If it gripped him with both arms he would be doomed. He heard the sound of it turning as he darted away again. He moved from side to side, touching it, taunting it, always out of reach.

The monster became maddened. It breathed in short, angry snorts.

"I'm here!" called Theseus.

He heard it coming, gauged the height of its head, reached out and seized a horn. With his free hand he drew the sword and thrust it blindly forwards, into flesh. He felt the Minotaur sag. He knew it was wounded, but still it came at him, bellowing in fury. He stabbed again with the sword, and this time the creature grunted, staggered and fell. Its breathing slowed. Theseus waited, his sword at the ready, while the shuddering breaths echoed in the labyrinth; but at last they stopped.

The Minotaur was dead. And now Theseus was alone at the heart of the labyrinth. In the struggle with the monster he had dropped the ball of thread; he cast about on hands and knees in the darkness, seeking it. When he had it in his hand again a great relief came over him, and a great longing for the light. Trembling, he began to rewind the ball, following, as he did so, the tortuous path back to the entrance.

He reached the door, and called softly, "Princess? Are you there?"

Then Ariadne, with the guard she had bribed, opened the door, and Theseus saw the light of day, the beautiful girl who had saved him, and the Athenian youths and maidens falling to their knees in gratitude.

"Come quickly!" said Ariadne. "Your ship is ready."

The company hurried out, down to the quay where the Athenian ship waited. Ariadne smiled as Theseus led her aboard. The crew hoisted the black sails and set a course for Athens.

* * * *

And so the youths and maidens of Athens were restored to their families, and in later years Theseus became famous as the hero who defeated the Minotaur.

But the voyage home was a long one, and on the way Theseus grew tired of Ariadne, and regretted promising to make her his wife. Halfway home they stopped at the island of Naxos to rest for a few days, to refill their casks with fresh water and to barter for bread, cheese and honey from the inhabitants. Theseus made up his mind to abandon Ariadne. One hot noonday, when the princess lay sleeping in the shade beside a stream, Theseus gathered his companions and crew and told them they must leave at once.

He left Ariadne asleep, and by the time she woke and looked for him, the black-sailed ship was far out at sea.

But Theseus, in his haste to leave Naxos, had forgotten his promise to his father that he would change the black sails for white if they returned victorious. Aegeus, hearing that the ship was sighted, hurried to a rocky headland to watch its approach. When he saw the black sails he believed his son was dead, and in his despair he threw himself into the sea and drowned.

ARIADNE
ON NAXOS

Ariadne, daughter of King Minos of Crete, lay sleeping in the shade on the island of Naxos.

When she woke, the sun was lower in the sky and a cool breeze blew. She stood up, looked around for her companions, and was surprised to find herself alone. Theseus rarely left her side, and the Athenian youths and maidens who had escaped with him from Crete could usually be found somewhere nearby.

Now all she heard was birdsong, bees busy in the flowers, the distant tinkle of goat bells. Puzzled, she set off along the path to the shore, calling the names of her friends as she went, and calling especially for Theseus, her love. But no one answered.

Perhaps they have gone to the ship, she thought; and she began to walk down to the bay where it was anchored.

Even before she reached the bay, she saw that the ship was gone.

Fear leapt up in her heart. Had Theseus moved to another anchorage? Was there danger? Had her father sent a ship in pursuit? She searched the shore, looking for a clue, a message. It was as if some god had removed, at a stroke, the ship and all the Athenians.

Headlands enclosed the bay, cutting off her view of the open sea. She began to climb, calling out as she went. Ahead of her a few goats scattered, kicking pebbles from under their hooves. Their cries echoed among the crags, but she heard no human voices. Her sense of unease increased.

And then, as she reached the highest point and looked out to sea, she saw what she had most feared: a ship sailing away from the island, its creamy wake cleaving the blue water; an Athenian ship with black sails.

"Theseus!" she cried. Panic overwhelmed her. She wanted to leap from the cliff and fly after him. "Theseus! Wait!"

But the ship was far off.

He cannot have forgotten me, she thought; he must think I am aboard.

And then she understood.

Theseus knew where she was. He had been sleeping beside her when they rested at noon. He had woken, gathered his companions about him, and left her. She had been abandoned.

Ariadne began to weep. She stretched out her arms towards the departing ship, crying out and begging Theseus to come back to her.

"I gave up my father's palace, my mother's care, for you!" she sobbed.

"I saved you from the Minotaur and yet you discard me as if I were some peasant girl…"

But Theseus could not hear her. The black-sailed ship, its course set for Athens, had dwindled to a speck on the sparkling sea. Ariadne called on the winds to change its course, but even they were against her; the ship sailed on. She sank to the ground in grief and shame, and covered her face with her hands.

And now, at last, she heard voices: loud voices, laughter, song – and music so joyous it seemed, at first, an affront to her distress. She looked up. A company of people was coming towards her across the rise of the headland. And what a company! Satyrs and nymphs led the way, piping and dancing. Behind them came a golden chariot drawn by two spotted leopards, and in the chariot stood a young man – surely a god? – of extraordinary, radiant beauty. His eyes were fixed on her. His long hair, entwined with a wreath of olive leaves, hung in golden ringlets. His tunic was bordered with gold, around his shoulders was the pelt of a lynx, and covering all was a purple cloak that swirled behind him and fell in soft folds as he halted his chariot.

Ariadne rose to her feet. She knew this must be Dionysus, the god of wine. Eros was there also, and Pan, and a host of revellers.

Dionysus stepped down from his chariot and approached Ariadne.

"Beautiful Ariadne," he said, "your lament has captured my heart. Dry your tears. Don't weep for that faithless Athenian; he is not worthy of you. You, princess, should be the bride of a god. I offer myself as your husband and lover. Forget Theseus; he is nothing compared to me. Is not a god, an immortal, preferable to one who will age and die? You shall have Olympus for your home, and as token of my love I will crown you with a coronet of stars."

Ariadne listened in wonder to this speech. The tears dried on her cheeks as she basked in the radiance of the immortal who offered her his love. Theseus, whom she'd loved and risked all for, was gone. He cared nothing

for her. But Dionysus had recognized her worth. She did not notice the arrow that Eros shot into her heart, but when Dionysus held out his hand to her, she stepped forward and took it.

* * * *

The wedding festivities began at once. Eros created a bridal chamber entwined with flowers: roses and lilies and sweet-smelling violets. For Ariadne he made a circlet of leaves and red roses, and as he placed it on her head she smiled and her eyes were bright once more. All around her, like birds, flew the winged Erotes who attend on marriage. Pan led the piping; the Graces filled the island with the scents and flowers of spring; the Hamadryads sang and all the nymphs and satyrs danced. As the marriage hymn was chanted, Ariadne entered the bridal chamber with Dionysus and became the wife of the god.

* * * *

Dionysus loved Ariadne. As he had promised, he gave her a golden crown set with nine jewels that sparkled like the stars of heaven. He took her with him to Olympus and set her among the gods.

Ariadne had several children; but she was mortal, and could not live for ever like her husband. When she died Dionysus was grief-stricken. He took her crown and cast it into the heavens, where its nine jewels blazed like fire and turned to stars. And there it remained, a circle of stars known as the constellation Corona, ensuring that Ariadne, though mortal, was never forgotten.

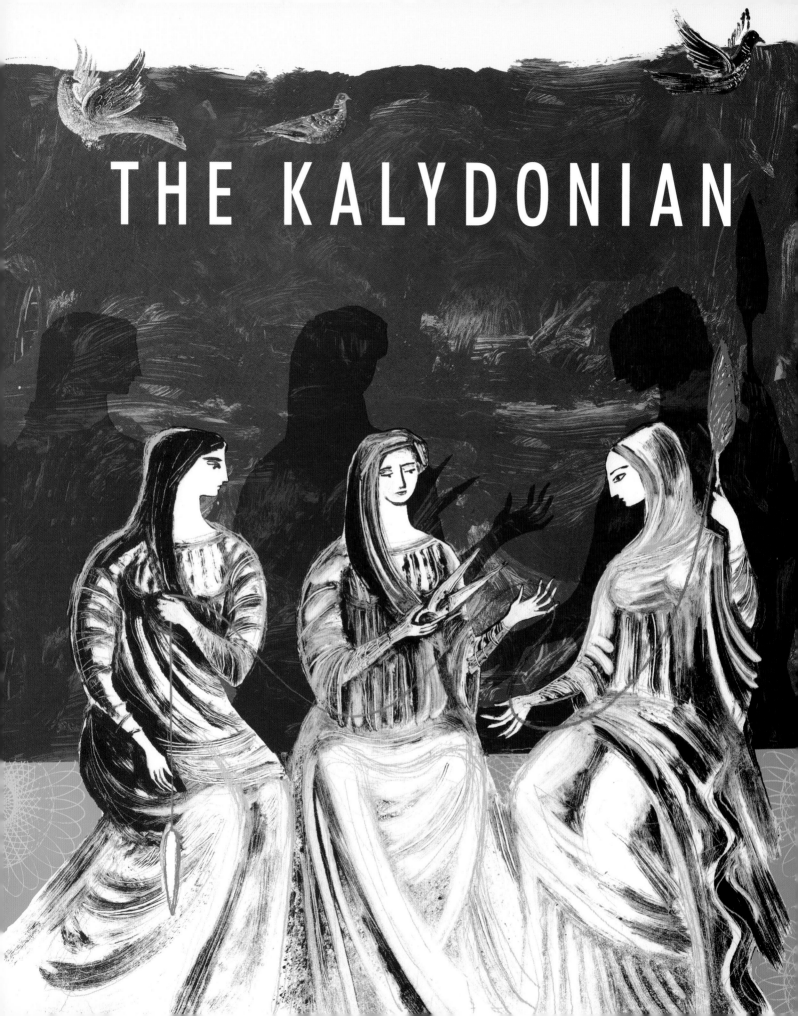

THE KALYDONIAN

BOAR HUNT

Oeneus, King of Kalydon, and his wife Althaea, had a son they named Meleager. When the child was a few days old, the three Moirai, the Fates, came to tell Althaea his destiny. As they stood spinning, drawing out with quick fingers the threads of his life, the mother watched with anxious heart. Then one of the Moirai pointed to the hearth, where a fire was blazing.

"This child," she said, "will live no longer than that log that burns in your hearth."

And with that the three women vanished.

Terror for her child gripped Althaea's heart. But she acted quickly. She seized the fire tongs and pulled out the log and smothered the flames with her cloak.

Then she took Meleager in her arms and kissed him.

I have outwitted the Fates, she thought. My child will live.

And Meleager did live. He grew up to be a brave, handsome young man, the pride of both his parents. He was a renowned warrior, and was one of those who accompanied Jason on the *Argo* in his quest for the Golden Fleece.

He never knew of the log, which his mother kept wrapped and hidden in a safe place where it could come to no harm.

One summer the lands around Kalydon had the best harvest that anyone could remember. It was a time of celebration. King Oeneus ordered the first sheaves of corn to be carried in procession and laid on Demeter's altars. The oil from the first pressing of olives was offered to Athena. Wine from the grape harvest was poured in honour of Dionysus, and there was dancing and music.

But Artemis, goddess of the hunt, received nothing, and was offended.

She sent a giant boar to ravage Kalydon: a creature of terrifying size, with bristles like spears, tusks that could rip up the earth, breath of fire, and eyes that caught every movement, so that no man could outwit it.

This boar burst upon Kalydon and destroyed the harvest. It trampled the corn, uprooted the olive trees, pulled down the grapevines and trod them into the earth. No one could stand against it. The shepherds tried bravely to defend their flocks, but the boar savaged the sheep with its great tusks and tossed the shepherds' dogs aside like rags. So many men died that at last all the people fled from the countryside to the safety of their walled city and called on the King for protection.

Meleager saw a way to destroy the boar and make a name for himself.

"Father," he said, "we have made sacrifices to the goddess and prayed for forgiveness, but it is clear that she will not relent. She means us to do battle with the boar. Let me send out a call for heroes to help

us defeat this beast. Jason will come, and those others who sailed with him on the *Argo*. We will organize a great hunt, and singers will tell of our deeds for generations to come!"

Oeneus agreed, and messengers were sent to all the surrounding kingdoms and cities: to Elis, to Olympia, to Athens, to Tegea in Arcadia, south to Sparta and Messene, and north to Iolcos.

The heroes came. Some were famous for throwing the javelin, some for boxing, some for horsemanship, some as warriors. Jason from Iolcos was there, and Theseus from Athens; the twins Kastor and Polydeuces, sons of Zeus and Leda; Peleus from Phthia; Meleager's two uncles, Plexippus and Toxeus; and many others, among them one woman, Atalanta, a princess of Tegea in Arcadia.

This Atalanta was a boyish-looking girl, simply dressed, her hair tied back in a knot. On her shoulder was an ivory quiver full of arrows, and in her left hand she carried a bow. In that company of men she looked about her with a fearless gaze. Meleager, though a married man, was fascinated by her.

The King entertained his guests at Kalydon for nine days, promising the victor the head and skin of the boar to carry home as his trophy. Some of the heroes objected to Atalanta, saying it would demean them to hunt with a woman and that she should be sent home; but Meleager insisted that she stay.

Next day the hunt began. The heroes split into groups and spread out across the countryside, calling to each other with horns. They spread nets to catch the boar if it ran; they unleashed hounds on its scent, and they followed its gigantic footprints. With so many tracking the beast, it was not long before they had it encircled in dense woodland. They began to close in.

The boar plunged into a deep, tree-filled ravine. Far below them the hunters heard the crashing and breaking of its passage through the woodland, its furious snorts and grunts. They began to clamber down. Meleager was close to Atalanta. At the bottom of the ravine they found themselves in swampy ground, full of tall reeds and purple irises. The mud sucked

* 75 *

at their feet, making it difficult to move fast. In the thick of the reeds they heard the boar snorting and trampling.

Then, in a rush, it broke out. Meleager saw its blazing eyes and great curving tusks. A spear flew past its side; another, thrown by Jason, overshot the beast; a third fell short. Meleager knew the angry goddess was at work, catching the weapons and sending them astray.

The boar was enraged. Flames burst from its throat. It charged, killing two men instantly. One was cut off at the knees by its tusks; one disembowelled. Another leapt to safety in a tree. Kastor and Polydeuces hurled their spears, but the boar was too fast and they missed. One of Jason's shots flew wide and killed a hound.

Then Atalanta let loose an arrow from her bow. It struck the beast below the ear and drew blood. The hunters cheered. Several rushed in for the kill but were trampled and gored by the boar.

Swiftly Meleager threw two spears. The first stuck in the earth; the second sank deep into the boar's side. The beast rose up, roared, twisted in agony; blood ran from its jaws. Meleager leapt upon it and cut it down with his sword. As the beast sank and died, Meleager stood on its back and raised his arms to receive the cheers of the hunters.

The trophy was his. The hunters set to work skinning the boar and, at the end, presented Meleager with the skin and head. It was fitting, they said, that the King's son should carry it home in triumph.

But Meleager turned to Atalanta. "No," he said, "it is not I who should

have the trophy but Atalanta. She struck the first blow and drew the first blood. The honour is hers."

And he stepped aside, and let the girl take his place.

Atalanta accepted the gift with graceful thanks.

But among the hunters an angry murmur arose. Meleager's uncle, his mother's brother Toxeus, stepped forward. "The honour belongs to you, to your family, not to this stranger – this woman!" he shouted.

And his brother, Plexippus, cried out, "If you will not take the

prize, we – your kinsmen – claim it for ourselves!"

Then the brothers made as if to seize the blood-stained head, and Meleager, in a fury at being thwarted, rushed upon Plexippus and thrust his sword into his body. A great groan went through the company as Plexippus fell dying. Toxeus, in horror, was too slow. Before he could draw his sword Meleager had turned upon him and struck him down beside his brother.

* * * *

The procession back to the walled city of Kalydon was one of triumph and grief. The King and Queen heard the wailing as the hunters approached, carrying the dead. A messenger ran ahead to break the news.

When Althaea heard that her own son had killed her two brothers, she wailed and tore her hair.

"Meleager is no longer my son," she said.

And she went to that secret place where, long ago, she had hidden the blackened log she snatched from the fire. She unwrapped it and found it still sound and strong, as if it might last forever.

She turned to her women. "Fetch wood for kindling."

When they brought the wood she would not let them make the fire, but lit it herself, feeding sticks and branches to it until the flames crackled and burned bright. Then she took up the log.

It held Meleager's life, and for that she gripped it to her body, unwilling to do what must be done. But Meleager had killed her brothers, his own kinsmen. His life was forfeit.

Twice she moved to throw the log on the flames, and twice drew back, unable to do the deed. Then she heard the keening of her daughters as the bodies of Plexippus and Toxeus were brought into the hall, and she grasped the log and flung it into the heart of the fire.

The log settled, and seemed to groan. Then flames engulfed the dry wood and began to consume it.

Outside the city, walking in procession with the hunters, Meleager felt a pain, like fire, grip him from within. Bravely he

continued to walk, but the burning spread, and grew hotter, as if he were being consumed by fire. At last he cried out in agony and fell to the ground.

His friends rushed to his side, but found no wound. Yet Meleager knew he was dying; and he grieved to die in such a way, and not in battle.

In Althaea's hearth the log crumbled to ash, and at the same moment Meleager's last breath left him.

When his body was carried into the city his father fell to the ground in grief. And his mother, seeing her dead son, took his dagger and plunged it into her heart.

Meleager's sisters were inconsolable. The goddess Artemis, her anger appeased at last, took pity on them, and turned them into birds, and set them free into the air.

ATALANTA'S RACE

Atalanta returned home to Arcadia in triumph, bearing the head and skin of the Kalydonian boar. She hoped to become famous as a hunter and follower of Artemis, but her father, King Iasos, had other plans for her. He wanted her to marry.

Atalanta had not been brought up as a princess. When she was born her father, who wanted only sons, had told her nurses to expose the baby on the mountainside. She was found and suckled by a she-bear, and later taken by hunters and raised as a woodsman's child. She learned forest lore, how to track animals, how to use a spear and a bow and arrow, how to run as swiftly as the deer; and she worshipped Artemis, goddess of the hunt.

As Atalanta grew up, word went around about the bold, boyish girl who had been found by hunters as a baby; and the King heard the stories and realized that this must be his own child. He had long regretted  his rejection of Atalanta. He sent for her, restored her to her rightful place as his daughter, and gave her every honour.

And now he wished her to marry. Suitors came regularly to the palace at Tegea, some of them wealthy princes from neighbouring kingdoms. A marriage between one of these and his daughter would increase King Iasos' power and influence.

Atalanta did not want to marry, but she knew that if she refused her father might force her to marry a man of his own choosing. So she set a condition.

"I will consent to be married," she said, "but only to the man who can out-run me in a foot race. And every man who loses must forfeit his life."

That would leave her free of suitors, she thought. But it did not.

The news spread around, and soon hopeful young men began to come to Tegea from all the surrounding kingdoms – not only princes but warriors and athletes, all drawn by stories of the wilful princess who could run like the wind.

Atalanta beat them all; and all paid with their lives. She began to believe that no man would win her.

But watching from the spectators' seats was a young man named

Hippomenes. He was an athlete, a renowned runner, and had been drawn to Tegea by stories of Atalanta's speed in the race. He had no intention of challenging her. He knew what became of those who failed, and he regarded them as poor fools, lured by a proud woman to a shameful death.

He watched Atalanta walk out onto the track and cast off her robe. Beneath it she wore a short tunic like a boy's, and her body was boyish, slender and straight. Her long hair was tied back and fastened with ribbon, and she wore coloured bindings at her knees and ankles, tied with bright ribbons that fluttered in the breeze.

Her competitor was a tall young man, strong-looking and long-limbed. He'd surely succeed, Hippomenes thought. But, as the race began, Atalanta at once took the lead and stayed there, running with ease, the ribbons at her knees and ankles streaming behind her. As she passed close by him, Hippomenes saw the rosy colour rising in her cheeks, her bright eyes glancing back, the effortless perfection of her running. He fell in love, and knew he must win her for himself.

But she was so fast! He was a champion runner, but he did not know if even he could out-run her. Before the day of the next race he prayed to Aphrodite, the goddess of love.

"Help me, great goddess!" he implored. "You have lit the fire of love in me. Help me to achieve my desire."

Aphrodite's heart was touched by his plea. She appeared beside him,

and he fell to his knees, overwhelmed by her golden beauty and the sweet scents that wafted around her.

"Rise up," said the goddess.

She gave Hippomenes three golden apples, and told him how to use them in the race. These apples were the most wonderful things Hippomenes had ever seen. They gleamed and sparkled and enticed the eye. No girl could resist them, Aphrodite promised.

On the day of the race Hippomenes stood beside Atalanta and felt his longing for her renewed.

As for Atalanta, she glanced sidelong at Hippomenes. For the first time she felt that she did not want this man to die; yet die he must, for her pride would not allow her to slow down, and she was certain that there was no man she could not beat.

Both competitors crouched at the starting place. A trumpet sounded: they were off! At first they ran level, at a steady pace; then Atalanta drew ahead. It was time for Hippomenes to act.

He took out the first of the golden apples, increased his speed and, as he passed Atalanta, rolled the apple across her path.

Atalanta saw it, and slowed. The apple gleamed and she longed to touch it. Hippomenes had begun to move ahead.

He thinks to trick me, thought Atalanta. I'll show him what I can do.

Swiftly she darted aside, picked up the golden apple, and sprinted after Hippomenes until they were level again. The crowd cheered and Atalanta

laughed in triumph. The delight of the crowd gave her new strength, and she passed Hippomenes and moved ahead.

But soon he was level with her again, and now another apple rolled past her feet. Atalanta, scarcely slowing her pace, ran and caught it, and passed Hippomenes again, while the crowd roared approval.

They were on the last lap now, and Hippomenes was tired. He struggled to keep pace with Atalanta, who still looked fresh and unhurried. It was time for the last golden apple.

He sent a prayer to Aphrodite as he threw it. The goddess made the apple heavier and sent it rolling far off the track and into the stony ground at the side.

Atalanta saw it roll, and knew it was too far off, but she could not resist the challenge. She turned and ran to retrieve it, picking her way in bare feet across the rough ground. She caught the apple, returned to the track and, with a final burst of speed, raced for the finish. But she had delayed too long. Hippomenes reached the finishing post, and raised his arms to receive the cheers of the crowd.

* * * *

Then Atalanta agreed to marry Hippomenes. And despite her determination not to marry, the two were happy, and might have stayed that way, had not Hippomenes forgotten to burn incense at Aphrodite's shrine and thank the goddess for her help.

The offended goddess set her heart against Hippomenes and his bride. One day the couple were visiting a shrine of Rhea, the great mother of all the gods. Aphrodite caused Hippomenes to feel a fire of passion for Atalanta, and the two made love in the temple, rousing the fury of Rhea. The great goddess turned them both into lions, and for ever after they were doomed to pull her golden chariot on its journeys around heaven and earth.

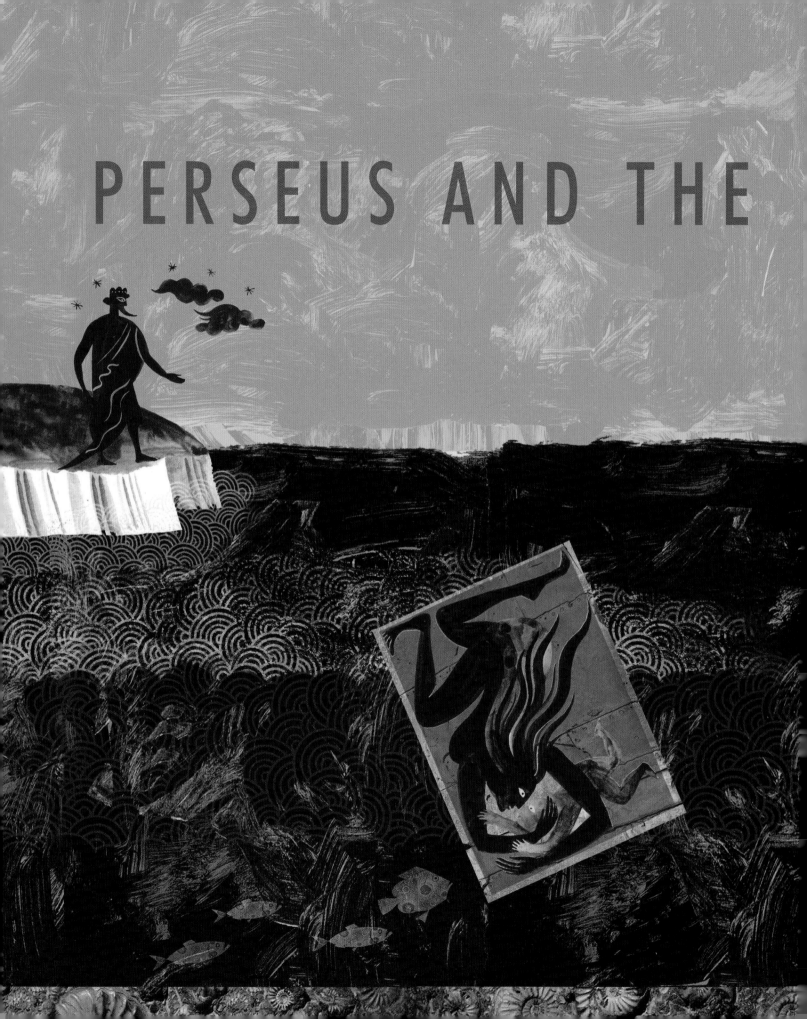

PERSEUS AND THE

GORGON'S HEAD

The King of Argos was warned by an oracle that his grandson would kill him, so he made up his mind never to have a grandson. He locked up his daughter Danae in a bronze room with only a small barred opening for light and air, so that no man could come near her.

But that could not keep out Zeus. The god turned himself into a shower of gold and poured into the stronghold. Nine months later Danae gave birth to a son, whom she named Perseus.

When her father realized what had happened, he shut up Danae and her son in a chest and threw it into the sea. The chest was washed up on the island of Seriphos and found by a man named Dictys, the brother of the King of Seriphos.

Dictys took care of Danae and Perseus and they lived in his house for many years, until Perseus had grown to be a young man. Throughout these years the King of Seriphos, Polydectes, pursued Danae for love; but although she refused, saying she could never love him, he continued to pester and waylay her. Only the watchfulness of Perseus prevented him from achieving his aim. The two men grew to hate each other, and Polydectes longed to be rid of Perseus, but since the youth was under his brother's protection there seemed to be nothing he could do.

Then came a day when Polydectes held a great feast and invited all the nobles and warriors of Seriphos. While the wine was flowing he asked his guests to say what would be the best gift for a king.

"A horse!" cried one, and all agreed, except Perseus. The youth, made reckless by wine, called out mockingly, "The head of a Gorgon!"

Everyone laughed, for no man could kill a Gorgon. The Gorgons were three sisters, monsters with bronze claws and wings and the tusks of beasts; anyone who met their pitiless gaze would be turned to stone.

The next day each of the nobles brought to the palace a horse as a gift for the king. Polydectes watched with pride and pleasure the procession of fine animals with their enamelled and jewelled bridles, saddles of the best workmanship, ribbons of gold and purple braided into their manes and tails.

Then he turned to Perseus – for he saw that his opportunity had come at last. "You have brought me no gift, Perseus. Yet you suggested one, I remember. I command you to bring me the head of a Gorgon!"

Danae gasped, and looked at her son in terror.

But Perseus, although he was afraid and regretted his rash words at the feast, said, "I will bring it."

That evening he prayed to Hermes and to Athena, and both gods appeared to him. They told him what he must do to succeed in his quest. First he must go to the cave where the Graiai lived. These were three withered women, grey-haired sisters of the Gorgons, who shared one tooth and one eye between them.

"They pass the eye and the tooth from one to another," said Athena. "You must steal the eye and keep it until they reveal to you the way to the Gorgons' country."

"The Gorgons..." said Perseus, and shuddered.

"Their names are Euryale, Stheno and Medusa," said Athena. "All are monsters but Euryale and Stheno are immortal and cannot die. Medusa is the one you must kill."

"Medusa. Forgive me, great goddess, how shall I know which is Medusa?"

"You will know her by her hair, which is not hair at all but a mass of writhing snakes that hiss and bite. Do not look at any of the Gorgons. I will lend you my bronze shield. Use it to reflect their images, and when you see Medusa, strike."

Hermes gave Perseus a curved knife of adamant and a pouch for the Gorgon's head. He lent the youth his own winged boots which enabled him to speed through the heavens, and his wide-brimmed cap that made the wearer invisible.

Perseus fell to his knees in gratitude and thanked the gods as they left him with these gifts.

Next morning he said goodbye to his mother and warned her to be wary of Polydectes. He strapped Hermes' winged golden boots onto his feet and put on the cap of invisibility. Then he flew, swift as the wind, to the cavern where the Graiai lived.

This cavern was in a cold, grey country, and he found the three withered women sitting around the embers of a fire. As soon as Perseus entered the cave they heard him.

"Someone is here!" cried one of the sisters. "Give me the eye! Give it!"

"Who's that? Who's there?" cried another.

Even the one with the eye could not see Perseus because he wore Hermes' cap. "Who has the eye?" the other two cried, stretching out scrawny arms.

"Deino has it. It's here."

And Perseus saw the hands, blindly reaching, and one that held the eye. He stepped closer, and took it.

The sisters began to quarrel.

"Where is it?"

"I gave it to you!"

"You dropped it!"

"No! You took it from me!"

Perseus stood clear of them and spoke. "I have the eye."

They gasped, and turned towards his voice. "Who are you? Give it back!"

"I have the eye," repeated Perseus, "and I will return it to you when you

tell me how to find your sisters, the Gorgons."

The Graiai muttered together. They were the guardians of the way to the Gorgons' country; it was their duty to keep out strangers. But what could they do without their eye?

"Listen," said the oldest of them. And she explained to Perseus how to reach the Gorgons. Then she stretched out a bony hand. "The eye!"

"The eye!" cried the other two.

Perseus returned it, and flew away, leaving them passing the precious item to and fro.

He knew he was in the land of the Gorgons as soon as he crossed its borders. It was rocky, parched and desolate, as the Graiai had described, and all around, on roads and plains, were still figures: people and animals turned to stone by the cold stare of a Gorgon.

Perseus felt afraid. There was no sign of life, only the statues, frozen in movement and with a look of terror on their faces. But as he flew onward he saw before him a cliff top, and on it perched what appeared to be three great birds with brazen wings. He held up Athena's shield and flew lower, tilting the shield to view them.

He saw that these were not birds, but female monsters. Their great gleaming wings enfolded them like cloaks as they perched, asleep, on a crag on the cliff top. Their bronze hands ended in sharp curving claws that gripped the rock. Their faces were turned away from him, half-hidden by their wings, but at any moment one might wake and look round. He dared only view their reflections in the shield.

He moved it to study each one in turn. The middle one was Medusa
– she of the snaky hair. He heard its faint hissing and saw the snakes'
tongues flicker in and out. Their many eyes gleamed. *They* were not
asleep. What if they woke Medusa? He knew he must act at once.

He crept closer, keeping Medusa's reflection in the shield. The snakes

became agitated. Close behind the monster Perseus stopped and drew Hermes' knife from its scabbard.

The scrape of metal alerted Medusa. She turned; he saw in the shield her terrible stare; and then he struck, and sliced off her head.

Blood spouted from the neck. Medusa's sisters woke and shrieked and rose on clattering wings as Perseus seized the head and stowed it in his pouch. They saw it disappear and, although he was invisible, they lunged, screaming in fury, their claws swiping the air around him. With the shield held up to protect himself, Perseus sped away. But the Gorgons heard him go. They flew after him, beating the air around him with their great wings. He watched them, reflected in Athena's shield, and quailed at the sight of their fierce teeth and claws. If they caught him, they would tear him to pieces before ever he was turned to stone.

But Hermes' winged boots took him high and fast into the heavens, and soon he was clear of the Gorgons' land and flying above the head and shoulders of Atlas. Atlas was the Titan who, for untold ages, had held up the heavens and all the stars. The weight of this burden crushed even his giant frame and he longed to be free of it, but he was immortal and would never die. When he heard Perseus approach he cried out, "Who's there?" and Perseus took off the cap of invisibility and told him about the Gorgon's head.

Then Atlas saw a way out of his plight. "Take pity on me," he said. "Let me look at the face of Medusa."

Perseus was reluctant, appalled, yet curious too, for he had never seen the transformation to stone take place.

He reached into the pouch and pulled out the head, being careful to hold it facing away from him.

Atlas stared at the dead face, and Perseus saw a greyness come over the Titan's features, and then cracks appeared; his shoulders sagged and settled, and his face changed and became craggy; his eyebrows were lines

of trees, and his eyes – were those eyes or dark cave openings? Where his hair and beard had been was dense forest. Atlas the Titan was gone. He had become the range of mountains that bears his name to this day.

Perseus flew on towards Ethiopia, and now, as he flew across the sea, he saw far below him a young woman chained to a rock below a headland. Waves were breaking at her feet. He flew lower, and the girl looked up and cried out to him for help.

"Who are you? Why are you here?" asked Perseus.

"I am Andromeda, the king's daughter." The girl explained that her mother, Kassiopeia, had boasted that she was more beautiful than the Nereids, the nymphs of the sea, and that as a punishment the Nereids had sent a sea monster to ravage the Ethiopian coast. Her father had sought help from an oracle, which told him that if he were to sacrifice his daughter to the sea monster it would go, and leave his people in peace.

As she stopped speaking, a look of terror appeared on the girl's face. She pointed out to sea. "It is coming for me!"

Perseus saw a ripple under the surface of the water, a long dark shape moving rapidly nearer. Andromeda screamed as the monster's head burst from the water, streaming weed and foam. It turned towards the sound, and its jaws gaped wide.

Perseus lunged downwards with Hermes' knife and struck the monster a deep blow in the shoulder. No ordinary blade could have pierced that scaly skin, but the god's knife was so sharp it could cut through stone. The creature howled and turned its jaws on Perseus, who flew upwards, out of its reach.

He struck again, darting down to stab, and then upwards to escape the monster's snapping teeth. Blood stained the sea and the monster grew more ferocious. As Perseus flew down to strike again it whirled around and lashed with its tail, so close it grazed his golden boot. Wounded but still dangerous, it turned its attention once more to the chained girl. Andromeda screamed.

"Look away!" Perseus warned her. "Close your eyes!"

And from his pouch he drew the Gorgon's head. He raced towards Andromeda and held the trophy up above the monster's snapping jaws.

The monster turned to see what Perseus held – and its jaws turned to stone. Perseus hid away the head, and when he looked again he saw that where the serpent had been was nothing but a ridge of rock breaking the surface of the sea.

The girl still stood with her head averted and eyes shut, shaking with fear. Perseus alighted beside her and said, "Princess, you are free."

With Hermes' knife he struck through the chains that bound her, and led her up the cliff to safety. Her parents were overjoyed to see her safe and asked Perseus how they could reward him.

"If the maiden is willing, I choose Andromeda as my bride," said Perseus.

The girl and her parents agreed. Then, on the shore, Perseus built three turf altars to the gods – Hermes, Zeus and Athena – and made sacrifices to them in gratitude before walking with Andromeda to the wedding feast in her father's hall.

But Andromeda's father had not told Perseus that his daughter had formerly been promised to another suitor, her uncle Phineus. This man, who had not troubled to try and save her from the sea monster, came now with warriors to take her away by force. A great battle ensued, and many of Andromeda's family took the part of Phineus because he was a kinsman. Those who supported Perseus were outnumbered, and although the youth fought bravely he found himself cornered and surrounded by enemies. Phineus moved in, his sword at the ready.

Perseus shouted a warning to his friends to look away. Once again he brought out the Gorgon's head and held it up. Phineus was stopped in mid-stride, his sword arm upraised, a triumphant smile frozen forever on his face. Behind him, several of his followers suffered the same fate; the others fled in terror.

And so, at last, the interrupted wedding feast took place. When it was over, Perseus and Andromeda travelled to Seriphos, where Perseus heard

that his old enemy, Polydectes, had abducted his mother and imprisoned his own brother, Dictys, who had tried to protect her.

Perseus strode into the king's hall, unwashed and bloody from his adventures, and faced Polydectes in front of his assembled warriors.

Polydectes gave a great laugh. "Well, if it's not young Perseus, back from his travels and looking the worse for wear! So, boy, have you brought me the Gorgon's head?" And he looked round at his followers, who all laughed with him.

For answer Perseus reached into Hermes' pouch and seized Medusa's head by its snaky curls. He pulled it out, still dripping blood, and before

Polydectes knew what was happening he had stared full into Medusa's terrible eyes. In an instant he and all his nobles were turned to stone.

Then Perseus freed Dictys, who became King of Seriphos and married Perseus' mother Danae, whom he had long loved.

Perseus returned the winged boots, cap, pouch and knife to Hermes, and the bronze shield to Athena. He made a gift of Medusa's head to Athena and the goddess set it in the centre of her shield.

Then Perseus and Andromeda went to his birthplace, Argos, to make peace with his grandfather; but the old man, hearing that Perseus was on his way, and remembering the words of the oracle, feared that his grandson had come to kill him. He fled to the land of the Pelasgians. Perseus became king of Argos in his stead and ruled it wisely for many years.

But what the Fates have decreed can never be averted. Perseus travelled one spring to a far country to take part in their public games. There he threw a discus which struck and accidentally killed his grandfather, who by chance was among the spectators. And so, at last, the oracle was fulfilled.

BELLEROPHON
AND THE
WINGED HORSE

Bellerophon was a prince of Corinth who was living under the protection of King Proetus of Tiryns. Proetus' wife fell in love with Bellerophon and made advances to him, but when he rejected her she became angry; she twisted the story around and told lies about him to her husband.

Proetus knew that honour required him to kill the young man. But he liked Bellerophon, and felt unwilling. Instead, he sent him to his wife's father, King Iobates of Lycia, with a letter of introduction. Unknown to Bellerophon, this letter asked Iobates to have the bearer put to death.

When Iobates read the letter he was shocked. He did not act on it immediately but entertained Bellerophon for several days in his palace. In that time he found him princely and courteous, and grew to like him. His daughter, Philonoe, looked with eyes of love at the young man, and

Iobates, knowing Bellerophon was a prince of Corinth, thought the match would be a worthy one.

And yet the letter troubled him. He could not bring himself to have Bellerophon put to death at Proetus' command, but neither could he ignore the request. He thought of a solution.

There was a monster, the Chimaera, ravaging parts of Lycia at that time, burning the land with its fiery breath and killing sheep. It was said to be a three-headed beast shaped like a lion but with a goat's head rising from its back and a serpent-headed tail that could sting with deadly venom.

"Only a hero could overcome the Chimaera," said Iobates. "Kill it, and you shall marry my daughter."

Bellerophon was afraid, though he did not show it; but Philonoe wept and begged her father to change his mind. "No man has ever fought the Chimaera and lived," she said.

Iobates knew that. He thought: either Bellerophon will kill the creature and prove himself a hero, or he will be killed, and I need no longer think about that letter.

* * * *

The night before he set off on his quest, Bellerophon went to the temple of Athena to pray for guidance, for he knew he could not kill the Chimaera unaided.

Athena heard his prayers and took pity on him. She caused him to sleep,

and he lay all night asleep in the temple. And there Athena sent him a dream of the winged horse, Pegasus.

This horse was born from the severed neck of the Gorgon Medusa, who was slain by Perseus. His great wings caused him to fly up into the air and race above the clouds. Athena had caught and subdued him, and taken him to live with the Muses on Mount Helicon. There, below the summit, he struck with his hoof, and from his hoof-print burst a spring of clear water that became known as the Hippocrene Spring.

No mortal had ever approached Pegasus, but Athena spoke to the dreaming Bellerophon and told him he should capture and tame the winged horse and use his power to overcome the Chimaera. And she gave him a golden bridle.

Bellerophon woke at dawn to find he was holding the bridle in his hand. It shone with a soft light in the dimness of the temple. He knew then that his dream was real, and that the goddess had answered his prayer. He resolved to find Pegasus.

There were several springs throughout Greece where the flying horse was said to come and drink, and Bellerophon knew that one was the Pirene Spring near his own home town of Corinth. He went there to wait for Pegasus.

* * * *

The Pirene Spring rose high in the mountains above Corinth. Bellerophon climbed the rough track and came upon it in a rocky place, sheltered by trees. There he saw the spring bubbling up. It formed a clear pool in a natural basin of rock from which it overflowed and ran down the mountainside into the city. Bellerophon hid himself among the trees and waited.

A long time he stayed there, the golden bridle loose in his hand. He watched the sky. It was bright and empty. He listened for hoof beats or wing beats, but all he heard were the rustle of leaves, the calling of birds, and the sound of the stream as it ran and rolled pebbles on its downward path.

And then, at last, in the cool before sunset, he heard great wing beats approaching, and he looked up and saw the winged horse flying towards him from the west. Pegasus was bigger and more godlike than Bellerophon had imagined; he shone gold and his wings seemed rimmed with fire as he slowly circled and came to rest beside the spring. He folded his wings and then, like any other horse, dipped his head to the water.

Bellerophon crept close. He knew he must act fast or Pegasus would sense him and fly away. With the bridle in his hand he ran and vaulted onto the horse's back.

Pegasus reared, snorted, rose up on his hind legs, then launched himself swiftly upwards. Bellerophon, clinging in terror, saw the earth far below him while the furious horse bucked and kicked and arched his back in his efforts to throw him off.

But Bellerophon had tamed horses before. He held fast, awaiting

his chance. When it came, he reached and thrust Athena's golden bit between the creature's teeth.

At once Pegasus was subdued. It was as if he knew the goddess commanded him. He circled back to earth and landed once more beside the spring, where Bellerophon slid from his back and let him drink and graze awhile. He spoke softly to the horse, and calmed him, and stayed beside him as the sun set and darkness covered the mountain.

The next day Bellerophon mounted Pegasus with ease and flew back to Lycia in search of the Chimaera.

He saw it from afar, on the lower slopes of Mount Kragos: a great swathe of burnt land and the beast roaming over it, uttering fierce cries. As they drew closer he saw sheep lying dead, and people in despair, driven from their burning homes.

Bellerophon had heard tell of this monster but had never seen it. Its size and appearance terrified him. Flames spouted from the lion's mouth, and the serpent-headed tail thrashed and hissed wickedly. When it saw the winged horse above it, the Chimaera shrieked and shot forth a burst of fire that scorched the air and sent Bellerophon and his horse rearing back and rising higher in the sky.

Bellerophon held the bridle. He spoke to Pegasus. "Softly, now. Be ready."

He was armed with a bow and arrow and a javelin. He drew an arrow from his quiver, set it to his bow, and took aim. The arrow flew, and sank

deep into the lion's side. The creature roared in pain and fury, and the goat's head poured forth flames; but Bellerophon let fly another arrow and struck it in the neck. The monster writhed in fury as Bellerophon urged Pegasus down closer for the kill. The serpent-headed tail whipped past his face and its tongue flickered. Bellerophon seized his javelin and thrust it into the flaming mouth of the lion's head. The flames were so hot that the lead tip melted and the creature suffocated. It sank down, choking, and the goat's and serpent's heads drooped and their eyes dulled. The Chimaera was dead.

Pegasus brought Bellerophon to earth, where he received the gratitude of the people of Mount Kragos. Then he mounted the horse again and they flew back in triumph to King Iobates' palace.

The King was astonished to see Bellerophon return alive – and unsure whether to be glad or dismayed. He sent him on another mission, this time to fight the Amazons. When Bellerophon once again returned victorious he saw that the youth must be under the protection of Athena. He looked kindly upon him and gave him his daughter Philonoe in marriage.

Bellerophon and Philonoe lived happily for many years, but Bellerophon, having found so much favour with the gods, began to believe himself almost their equal. He called upon Pegasus once more, and urged the winged horse higher and higher into the air, intending to reach Olympus, where the gods lived. But Pegasus reared and threw him, and he tumbled down through the wastes of air and was killed.

As for Pegasus, he went to live in the stables of Zeus on Olympus. And Zeus set him among the stars, where he can still be seen as the constellation of the Horse.

GODS

AND

MORTALS

PAN AND SYRINX

While the god Hermes, the luck-bringer, was in Arcadia he fell in love with a nymph, the daughter of Dryopos, and to win her he took the disguise of a shepherd and worked for her father, helping to tend his sheep. Before long he married the nymph and she gave birth to a son, the god Pan.

When the nurse who delivered Pan saw the child she screamed and ran from the house in terror: for Pan was born with goat's feet and hairy legs, two little horns on his forehead, and a beard. But he was a noisy, happy child, and Hermes loved him. He wrapped him in the warm skins of mountain hares and carried him to Olympus to show him to the gods. He set him down beside Zeus, and the baby laughed, and all the gods were delighted with the strange child, and all loved him – especially Dionysus, the god of wine.

Pan became the shepherds' god, roaming the wooded crags and deep gorges and tumbling rivers of Arcadia. He knew every mountain crest and the course of every stream. His joy lay in hunting wild beasts, and he would race in pursuit of them, leaping sure-footed from crag to crag on his goat's feet. At midday or evening he would stop and rest by some cool stream or in a meadow full of hyacinths, and there he would lie and listen to the voices of nymphs in the woodland.

Pan often pursued nymphs for love, and only those who were wary and fast escaped him. One such was Syrinx, a beautiful Naiad, famous among the nymphs of Nonacris. Syrinx refused all offers of love. She was a follower of Artemis, and might have been taken for the goddess herself except that her bow was made of horn while the goddess's was gold.

When Pan saw Syrinx he immediately fell in love with her; the nymph fled, and he gave chase. Syrinx was fast, but when she reached the banks of the river Ladon she fell exhausted, like the beasts she so often hunted, and cried to her watery sisters, the Naiads of the river, to change her.

Pan leapt and seized the nymph – but all he held in his arms was a bunch of the tall marsh reeds that grew beside the river. He sighed, and the breeze blowing through the reeds sighed too, and sent out a plaintive sound.

Pan was captivated. The note came again, pure and piercing.

"Syrinx, you and I shall make music together!" cried the god.

And he cut reeds and trimmed them to different lengths so that each

made a different sound when he blew through it; then he bound them together to form a set of pipes known ever since as a syrinx.

So Syrinx never became a bride, but she sang at many a wedding, and Pan's pipes were often heard by shepherds as they minded their sheep on the high hillsides.

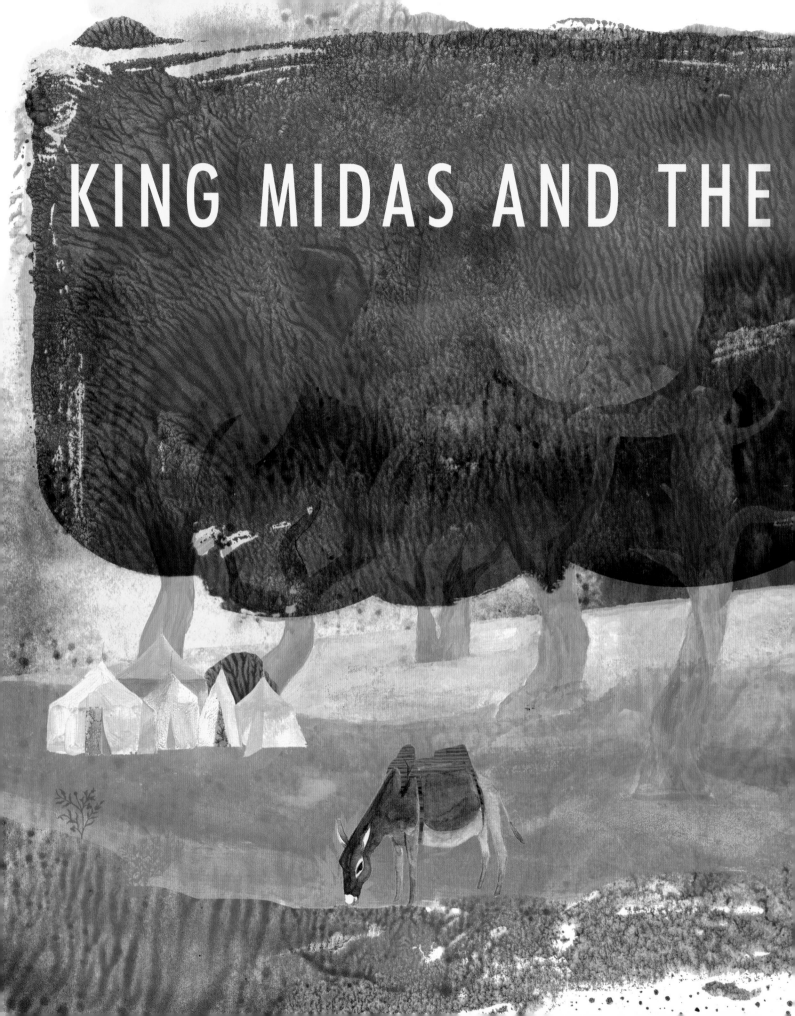

KING MIDAS AND THE

GOLDEN TOUCH

Dionysus, the god of wine and revelry, always kept about him a company of satyrs, nymphs, bacchantes and maenads. He travelled in his golden chariot, drawn by two leopards with shining reins, and wherever he stopped there was merry-making. The satyrs would play their pipes, the nymphs dance and sing.

One of Dionysus' dearest friends was Silenus, an elderly satyr, bald and fat, with ass's ears and a donkey's tail. He had once been a tutor to Dionysus and the god loved him.

One summer evening, when Dionysus and his company had set up camp on their way to the vineyards of Phrygia, the god realized that Silenus was missing. The old satyr's donkey – the one he always rode – ambled along, riderless, and Silenus was nowhere to be seen.

"Where is Silenus?" Dionysus asked.

But everyone was drinking wine, eating figs and honey, playing music on reed pipes. No one knew. No-one had seen what happened to Silenus.

★ ★ ★ ★

Meanwhile, Silenus woke up feeling dazed. He had fallen asleep, toppled off his donkey into a ditch and been knocked unconscious. When at last he managed to clamber out onto the roadside there was no sign of Dionysus and his company.

Some Phrygian peasants were coming along the road, walking home from the fields in the late afternoon. They saw Silenus staggering about and laughed.

"Hello, Grandad! Had a drop too much?"

Silenus tried to muster his dignity. "I am an immortal," he said, "one of Dionysus' company. But I fear I'm lost."

"Oh! A lost immortal!" Still they mocked him.

"When I was young, you know," said Silenus, "I was the god's tutor. Many were the hours we sat together…"

The peasants made him a crown of flowers and led him along the road, laughing at his rambling talk. They took him to their king, Midas, who always liked to have something new to amuse him.

But King Midas had met Silenus before. He recognized him and knew his story was true. Instead of laughing at him he received the old satyr with honour and ordered a great feast to be held, and made merry with him for ten days and nights. Meanwhile he heard that Dionysus was at one of his favourite haunts: the vineyards that clung to the lower slopes of Mount Tmolus in Lydia, above the valley of the river Pactolus. To that place, on the eleventh day, he travelled with Silenus and found the god encamped with all his entourage.

Midas approached cautiously, dazzled by the splendour of the god.

But when Dionysus saw that the king had brought Silenus to him he was overjoyed. He threw his arms around the old satyr, and cried to Midas, "Choose a reward! Anything! I will grant your heart's desire!"

His heart's desire... Midas pondered – but not for long enough. He was already wealthy beyond the dreams of other men, and his wealth gave him pleasure; so what could be better than more wealth, more pleasure?

"Grant that everything I touch will turn to gold," he said.

The god's smile faded. "This is a bad choice," he said. "Choose again."

But Midas would not budge. "That is my heart's desire," he said.

And so the wish was granted.

Midas went home. He went first to his garden, and cautiously touched a twig. Instantly it became a stem of gold. He picked up a pebble: a golden nugget lay heavy in his palm. He touched the seed-head of an ear of grass, and it became a delicate plaited chain.

Midas laughed in delight. This was wonderful; amusing. Why had the god hesitated?

The king's garden was famous for its roses. They were in bloom and their perfume scented the air. Midas sniffed one, and brushed its soft petals with his fingers. At once it turned to gold: a gleaming toy with perfect sculpted petals, unscented, unmoving. Midas felt his first flicker of doubt. But he had a garden full of roses that shed their fragrance on the breeze. And shed their petals too – unlike this rose, which would never die.

He picked it, and carried it into the palace. He laid his hand on the wall of his palace and saw the entire building flush with gold and blaze in the evening sun. All around, people gasped in amazement.

He was dusty, hungry and thirsty after his travels. A girl brought a basin of scented water for him to wash in, but at the first touch of his hand the water became a solid block of gold.

"Take it away," he said. "I will eat first."

His servants had prepared a great feast, and he approached the table eagerly. There were bowls filled with apples, grapes and pomegranates; dishes of roast meat; loaves of bread baked in braided patterns. He took a slice of meat, and felt it grow hard in his hand; he tried to bite it, and bit on flakes of gold.

A slow terror began to grow in him.

"Wine!" he cried. "To wash away this curse!"

A serving man filled his glass with wine, but when he raised it to his lips the red wine turned gold and hardened, and he sat spitting nuggets of gold onto the table and crying out in despair.

His people tried to help. The serving man lifted bread to the king's lips, but as soon as it touched them he was biting on gold again. A woman brought plain water, but even that turned to gold at his touch.

Then Midas knew that he would die of his foolishness, and he threw up his arms and cried, "Forgive me, Lord Dionysus! Set me free from your gift!"

Dionysus heard him, and relented. After all, he'd wanted to reward Midas, not to hurt him.

"Return to the River Pactolus, below Mount Tmolus," he said, "where we met. Climb upstream until you reach the source, and there immerse yourself in the pool where the water springs from the mountain. It will wash my gift away."

Midas thanked the god and followed his advice. He travelled to Lydia, climbed the steep mountainside to the river's source, and plunged in. The gift dissolved and flowed from him in streams of gold and ran glittering down the mountainside. Midas, trembling and fearful, stepped out of the water. He touched a twig, and then a rock; and when the twig remained wood and the rock remained stone he fell on his knees and thanked Dionysus for his mercy.

King Midas went home. But the River Pactolus still ran gold, and ever since that time people have found flecks of the precious metal in its shallows.

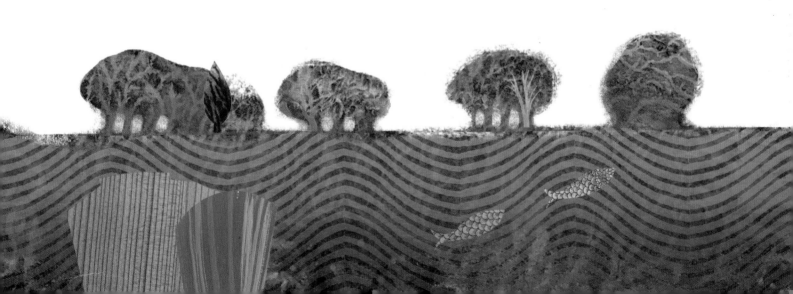

KING MIDAS AND THE

MUSIC CONTEST

After he returned from the River Pactolus, washed free of the gift of gold, King Midas declared that he cared no more for wealth; he was off to the wild woods and mountains to live on nuts and berries and become a follower of the god Pan.

His courtiers, who knew their master well, sighed and prepared to run the country until he came to his senses again. Meanwhile, King Midas left, feeling free as air, and followed the sound of Pan's piping.

And what piping it was! High-pitched, sweet, insistent, it echoed from the deep shade of caves high in the mountains, and was carried on the breeze with the warm scent of thyme and the buzzing of bees. It mingled with the rush of waterfalls, the rolling of pebbles in streams, the voices

of nymphs and birds. It drew Midas into the heart of the mountains and taught his feet to dance.

Pan played this sweet music on the reed pipes he had made after Syrinx escaped his grasp. He became so enamoured of his own music that he boasted that his playing was sweeter than Apollo's. This was unwise. Apollo was a great god, an Olympian, the god of music and prophecy. His music was peerless. Yet Pan, playing and dancing goat-footed on

the slopes of Mount Tmolus, challenged Apollo to a contest.

Tmolus, who was both the mountain and its god, was to be the judge. When Pan and the nymphs danced and hunted on those wooded slopes they saw only the mountain with its crags and streams. But now, as he prepared to give his judgement, a rugged shape appeared at the top of the mountain. It was old Tmolus himself, who rose, brushed aside trees and shrubs, shook the leaves out of his ears, and prepared to listen.

His voice echoed in the nymphs' caves: "Let the contest begin!"

Then Pan, the sunburnt goat god with a spotted lynx pelt slung over his shoulders, began to play. His music charmed the mountain, and drew King Midas and the nymphs to clap and dance. Pan sprang from rock to rock and led them down to meadows full of flowers where they leapt and laughed and cried out for more as the last notes died away.

Now Tmolus turned, with a rustle of treetops, to Apollo.

The great god shone with the radiance of Olympus. His hair hung in scented curls to his shoulders and was crowned with a wreath of laurel leaves. His cloak of Tyrian purple fell in opulent folds to his feet. His lyre was gold, inlaid with ivory and set with precious stones that flashed as they caught the light. He held the plectrum in his right hand and began to play.

Tmolus and the nymphs, and even Pan himself, grew still and silent. All nature seemed to hold its breath. The music that Apollo brought forth from his lyre was so pure, so perfect, that Pan's, in comparison, seemed nothing but a shepherd's romp.

When it was done, the nymphs breathed out all together with a sigh. The judge awarded the contest to Apollo, and everyone who heard agreed: the nymphs, the satyrs, the humbled Pan. All praised Apollo. Only King Midas dissented.

"I disagree," he said. "I liked Pan's music best."

Apollo, who had not even noticed Midas until then, turned on the king his immortal gaze. Midas quailed beneath it.

"Those undiscerning ears of yours, Midas," said the god, "should not have human shape."

Then Midas, to his alarm, felt his ears begin to change. He put up a cautious hand. His ears were growing! They felt huge – huge and floppy, and filled with rough hair! He ran and found a pool, and stared in horror and shame at his reflection. Apollo had given him ass's ears.

Midas fled to his palace. He gave up the woodland life for good. He had a special hat made to cover his ears and was never again seen without it – except by his barber.

This man carried the burden of the king's secret – for what use is a secret if you can't tell it? The barber longed to tell, but he was sworn to silence, on pain of death.

One day the secret became too much for the barber to bear. He went out to a field at the back of his house and dug a hole and whispered into it, "King Midas has ass's ears." Then he filled in the hole and went home, feeling better.

But when spring came, a crop of small green shoots emerged from the earth that the barber had patted down. They grew into a clump of reeds, and by full summer they were standing tall to catch the breeze.

The wind blew, and the reeds swayed and brushed together and whispered, and their whispering was carried all around: "Ass's ears… King Midas… King Midas has ass's ears…"

And so the secret was out.

ARACHNE

Arachne was famous throughout her homeland of Lydia – yet she was neither an immortal nor even a lady of noble birth. Her father was a humble dyer who lived and worked in the little town of Hypaepae, dyeing wool in rich colours of russet, yellow, green and, most prized of all, Phocaean purple.

From her mother, who was now dead, Arachne had learned the craft of weaving, and the girl had so far surpassed other women with her skill that people came from all over Lydia to watch her at work. Not only were her creations beautiful but she worked swiftly and with such grace and confidence that she was a joy to watch. She carded and spun all her own wool, pulling out threads from the mass on the distaff and twirling the spindle, drawing the spun wool through her fingers till it formed a fine, smooth yarn.

Her designs were planned in her head, and she brought them to life on the loom: scenes of hunting, feasting and celebration; trees and flowers; birds, cattle, cats and dogs so lifelike that people said they half expected them to jump off the loom. Even the Dryads of Mount Tmolus and the Naiads of the golden stream of Pactolus (where King Midas washed off Dionysus' gift) would often leave their homes and come to watch Arachne.

Such a gift could come only from the goddess Athena, yet Arachne denied this and often boasted that if she were to enter a contest with the goddess she would be sure to win.

Athena heard her, and was angry. She disguised herself as an old woman, grey-haired and leaning on a stick, and came to Hypaepae, where nymphs and women led her to Arachne's house. She watched Arachne at work and afterwards said to her, "You have great skill, my dear, but listen to one who is older and has seen more of life. Don't be proud. Enjoy the praise of mortals, but give honour to the goddess. Ask pardon of her for those unwise words of yours. She will give it freely if you ask."

Arachne tossed her head and laughed at the advice. "Why should I listen to an old woman whose brain has gone soft? Go and pester your daughters and your sons' wives! I take back nothing I said. Let Athena come herself – if she dares!"

Then the goddess threw off her disguise and said, "She is here!"

The nymphs and women fell to their knees, overcome with awe and terror as Athena's shining presence lit up the room. Arachne gasped and stepped back. She was afraid, but would not show it.

"Arachne," said the goddess, "do you stand by your challenge?"

And Arachne, too proud to give way, replied, "I do."

The contest began at once. Athena set up her loom beside Arachne's. Each weaver fixed her warp threads in place and pushed between them a rod to divide the strands and make a space through which the shuttle could pass. Each chose

her colours: soft shades of blue and tawny red, saffron yellow, green and kingly purple, to be mixed here and there with fine strands of golden wire.

Then both began to weave. Arachne, watching the goddess from the corner of her eye, kept pace with her. Her shuttle flew from side to side; the pictures in her mind grew in glorious colour on the loom as she worked. The crowd of nymphs, neighbours and other women gazed in amazement at the speed and skill of the two weavers, at their blending of colour, and the images – bulls, birds, monsters, gods, maidens, trees and flowers – that sprang to life on their looms.

Arachne had no time to look at Athena's work. All her attention was on her own design. She knew it was her best ever. Never before had she

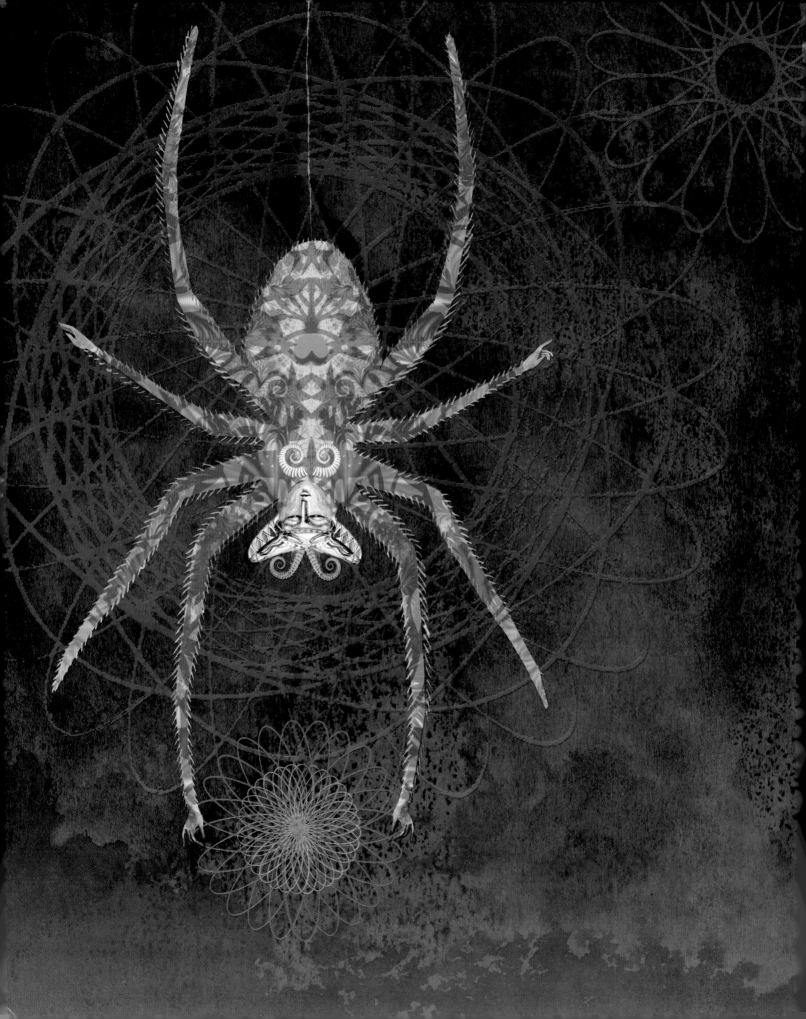

created such harmony of pattern and colour, such lively pictures drawn from life. As it grew, the work filled her with pleasure and pride.

But when at last both weavers finished, and Arachne turned to look at what was on her rival's loom, she saw there a perfection that only a goddess could achieve. Her own work, which had so delighted her, was nothing by comparison. All her joy in it was gone. She did not need to hear the verdict of the onlookers. She ripped her cloth from the loom and tore it. Then, in her shame and despair, she flung a strip of cloth over a beam and put a noose around her neck to hang herself. The women gasped and moved forward.

But before they could reach her the goddess cried out in a great voice, "Live, Arachne! Hang you shall, but you shall also live and weave – and all your descendants after you!"

Then Arachne, still hanging, began to shrink and change shape; and the thread she hung from shrank and became finer and finer. Arachne darkened and shrivelled until she was a tiny round creature; instead of four limbs she had eight little legs, all busily weaving the silvery thread she spun from her own body.

Arachne had become a spider. She is still a weaver, and her work can be seen to this day.

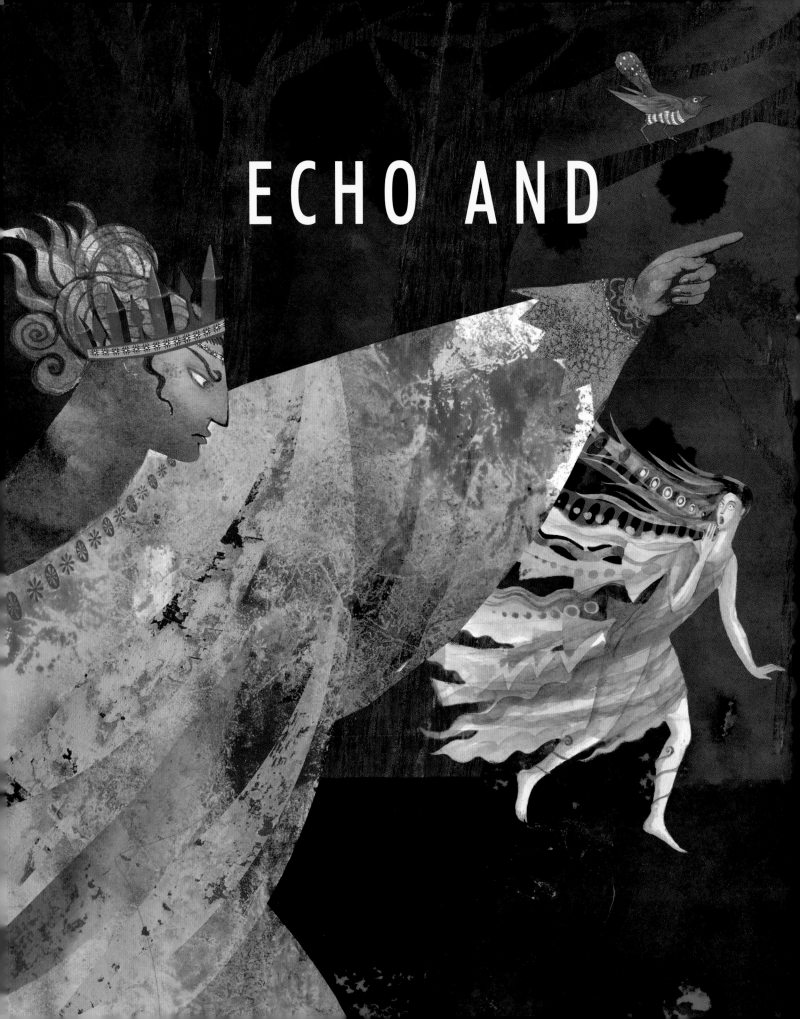

ECHO AND

NARCISSUS

Among all the nymphs of Boeotia who served the goddess Hera, Echo was known for her constant chatter. She heard all the latest gossip and would keep the nymphs and the goddess amused with her stories of loves and quarrels, of secrets and misunderstandings.

Zeus, the husband of Hera, found Echo a useful ally. He often deceived his wife and dallied with both nymphs and mortals, and many times Hera might have caught him had not Echo detained the goddess with her chatter.

When Hera found out how Echo had been tricking her, she was furious. She told the nymph, "Since you like to repeat what you hear, you shall do that – and nothing more." And she took away Echo's power of speech and condemned her for ever to repeat the last few syllables of anything that was said to her.

"Now leave my company. Be gone!" the goddess commanded.

And Echo, unable to beg for mercy, could only cry, "Gone!"

"Oh, Echo! Alas!" cried the nymphs.

"Alas!" repeated Echo.

Banished by the goddess, and unable to talk to her friends, the nymphs, she went to live in a cave high in the mountains. But Echo was lonely.

She would follow shepherds or hunters and try to join in their talk. She longed for company.

One day, as she wandered among the trees on the mountainside, repeating the calls of a group of hunters, she saw a young man who had become separated from his companions. This was Narcissus, the son of the river god Kephisos and the blue-haired water nymph Liriope.

Echo watched him as he wandered deeper into the

woodland. She fell in love with the beautiful youth, not knowing that Narcissus was proud and hard-hearted. Many girls and youths had offered him their love, but he would have none of them and held himself apart.

Echo kept close to him in the undergrowth, hiding because she knew she could never speak and declare her love, but only repeat whatever he said.

Narcissus, anxious to find his companions and rejoin the hunt, heard her moving nearby and called out, "Is anyone here?"

"Here!" cried Echo.

"Who are you?"

"Who are you?"

"Narcissus."

"Narcissus!"

"Come this way!"

"This way!"

Narcissus heard the branches rustle and turned towards the sound. "I'm here!" he said. "Come and join me!"

"Join me!" cried Echo, overjoyed – and she broke from her hiding place and ran towards him, holding out her arms.

At sight of her, Narcissus drew back. He curled his lip and said, "Be gone, nymph! Why do you follow me? I could never love *you*."

"Love *you!*" pleaded Echo.

But he had turned his back on her.

Echo, despairing and ashamed, went to hide herself in her cave. There she wept and could not be comforted. She wasted away; her body dried and became air, and all that was left of her was her voice and her bones. In time even her bones turned to stone, but her voice remained, and travellers hear it still in caves and wells and rocky places.

As for Narcissus, he continued to spurn all love, until one day a rejected nymph prayed that he might suffer for love as she had done – and the goddess Nemesis, who punishes pride, heard her.

Narcissus, out hunting and hot from the chase, came upon a pool. Trees and tall grasses grew around it, and the water was still, clear as polished silver, and pure. He lay down beside it and cupped his hands to drink. But as he leaned out over the water he saw below the surface a beautiful face: fine eyes, dark curling hair, a perfect neck and shoulders – some spirit of the pool, he thought, looking up at him.

"Who are you?" he asked – and the lips moved in silent reply.

Fired by love, Narcissus tried to kiss the lips, but they disappeared as soon as he touched the water.

When the pool grew still again the lovely creature returned. Narcissus reached out his arms, implored its love, and saw arms beneath the water reach out to him. But when he tried to embrace the spirit, it disappeared again.

"Don't leave me!" begged Narcissus.

All thought of food and drink now left him. He lay stretched beside the pool, gazing in longing at his own reflection, not knowing it to be himself, for Nemesis had taken away his reason. Over and over he

plunged his arms into the water, and every time the image eluded him.

Now Narcissus knew rejection. "How can you not love me," he demanded, "when so many nymphs have pined for my love?"

So he lay and wept, and at last, like Echo, he began to fade away.

"Alas!" he whispered. "Farewell!"

Echo answered him "Farewell!" and all the nymphs of woodland and water wailed with her as he died.

They say the Naiads came to bury Narcissus, but could find nothing there, not even bones – only a flower to which they gave his name.

PANDORA

In the beginning of the world, the gods of Olympus created men and animals. They set the Titan brothers Prometheus and Epimetheus the task of giving to each of the new creatures of the world its own special qualities.

First of all, Epimetheus made the choices for the birds and animals. Some he made strong but not swift, others fleet of foot but timid. Some were given cunning, some armour, others winged flight, or the means to make burrows in the earth. Some creatures he made large for their own safety, others tiny so that they could hide. He gave them also protection from sun, rain and wind: thick fur, or dense feathers, or leathery skin, or hooves to protect their feet. He made them all in such a way that every creature had the means to defend itself and no race of creatures could entirely destroy another.

Epimetheus was generous, but he did not think ahead; and when he had distributed gifts to all the birds and animals of the earth, he found that there were none left for Prometheus to give to men. Men were naked, without hairy covering, without shoes, and with no means of defending themselves.

When Prometheus saw what had happened he went up to heaven

and stole from the Olympians the art of making fire. This gift gave men the means to live and also mastery over all the animals. But the gods were angry with Prometheus. They planned to punish him with a gift which was also a snare.

Until that time men had lived without women. Now Zeus asked Hephaestus, the smith god, to create the first woman. Hephaestus mixed clay and water and breathed life into the form of Pandora, whose name means "all gifts". Each god gave her gifts. Aphrodite gave her grace and beauty; Athena taught her the arts of needlework and weaving, and clothed her in a wondrous embroidered veil. The Kharites decked her with golden necklaces and the Horai crowned her flowers. Hermes gave her the gift of speech and with it the power to lie and deceive.

The gods sent Pandora to earth as a gift to the two Titans, but Prometheus would not accept the gift, and he warned Epimetheus against Pandora.

"Be wary of any gifts the gods send," he said. "They may bring trouble."

But when Epimetheus saw the lovely Pandora he could not resist her, or believe that one so beautiful could be a danger to mankind. He took her as his wife and she made his home sweet with her womanly arts.

But Hermes had given Pandora a restless, inquisitive mind. In the storeroom of Epimetheus' house was a great stone jar set into the floor.

It was quite plain, with no markings on it, and was closed tightly with a stone stopper.

"What is in the jar?" Pandora asked her husband.

Epimetheus did not know. "The gods gave it to me for safekeeping at the beginning of the world. They warned me not to open it."

Pandora stared at the closed jar. "But – don't you want to see inside?"

"No doubt it contains some gifts or powers that were never required," said Epimetheus. He had no curiosity. The world, it seemed to him, was a good place, and whatever was in the jar, he had no need of it.

But Pandora could not leave the jar alone. She came back to it day after day and puzzled over what it might contain. She listened at the jar; she sniffed it; she knocked with her knuckles on the side. She would have shaken it, except that it was too big and was wedged firmly in the earth floor.

Gradually all her attention became centred on the lid. This was a heavy stone stopper that had been dropped in place to fit closely into the neck of the jar. It was neither sealed nor locked. All she had to do to see inside was to lift it.

At first she pestered her husband. "Just a quick peep!" she begged. "The gods won't know." But when she realized that he would not agree to open it, she became secretive. She would get up in the dead of night and light a lamp and go and look at the jar, and wonder, and sometimes close her hand around the knob on the lid to feel its weight and almost, almost, begin to lift it.

One night the temptation became too much for her. She put her hand on the lid, thinking: I'll raise it a little, just enough to peep, and then quickly put it back. And slowly, with a scrape of stone on stone, she lifted the stopper up until it cleared the rim of the jar. She was about to peer in when out of the darkness inside came a rush of wings, a shrill shrieking, a beating and buffeting and howling. Pandora dropped the lid and screamed in terror as the lamp was blown out and the dark room filled with noise and movement. Unseen things brushed past her, things that stung and scratched and tore at her hair and howled to be let out.

Epimetheus came running, woken by her scream, and the lamp in his hand lit up the whirling

creatures: winged spirits with cruel faces and sharp claws. He tried, with Pandora, to gather and sweep them back into the jar, but the task was impossible. The spirits flew out of the open door into all the rooms of the house and out through the windows into the world outside. As the sun came up, Epimetheus and Pandora saw the creatures she had released winging their way across the world.

Until then people had lived like the gods, free of pain, old age and death. The spirits that Pandora had set free were all the ills that have since plagued mankind: sickness, suffering, poverty, strife, discord, envy, war and despair.

Now Epimetheus understood how foolish he had been in accepting a gift from the gods. Pandora had brought harm to mankind. But when the two of them returned to look at the jar, they found it was not empty after all. One spirit remained – a gentle, sweet-faced one. This was Hope.

Hope stayed in the world of men, bringing comfort to people when the troubles of their lives became too hard to bear – and she remains in our world to this day.

To Maika and Dominic
Ann Turnbull

For my parents – V.Y and N.B.Y
Sarah Young

First published 2010 by Walker Books Ltd
87 Vauxhall Walk, London SE11 5HJ

2 4 6 8 10 9 7 5 3 1

This book has been typeset in Avenir

Printed in China

British Library Cataloguing in Publication Data:
a catalogue record for this book is available from the British Library

ISBN 978-1-4063-0083-3

www.walker.co.uk